# Wildlife Gardening

A practical handbook

by Fran Hill

Published by
Derbyshire Wildlife Trust

The Derbyshire Wildlife Trust
is one of 46 across the UK,
working in partnership as
The Wildlife Trusts

*Text and garden plans by Fran Hill*

*Illustrations by Daniel Rodrigues,
Jackie Farrand, Stephen Carroll, Jonathan Kear,
David Hands and Roderick Dunn*

*Photographs by Roger Barnes, Robert Hawksworth, W. J. Furse,
D. Martin, Peter Smith and Colin Varndell*

*Revised by Fran Hill, Nick Brown, Stephen Carroll, Helen Harris
and Derek Hilton-Brown*

*Compiled and edited by Nick Brown*

First published by Derbyshire Wildlife Trust, Elvaston Castle, Derby DE72 3EP in 1988



(Trust re-locating in 2001, please check address)

Revised and updated autumn 2000

ISBN 1 871444 00 4

Typeset and Printed by J. M. Tatler & Son Ltd., Abbey Street Works, Derby

# Introduction

WILDLIFE gardening is very much in vogue. At last it seems that more and more people are giving up chemical gardening and actively encouraging wild plants and animals into their gardens.

The pleasure to be derived from feeding birds during the winter is well known but there is so much more that can be done to attract a range of wildlife throughout the year, even if you live in a town.

A small pond will soon be inhabited by frogs, pond skaters and water beetles. Many species of butterfly will scent your nectar-rich flowers and call in for a drink. A show of cowslips or poppies will bring back memories of a countryside long since disappeared.

First though, you need to know what to do and how to do it. This book gives you the technical and practical help you require, from making and siting a nest box to planning a complete wild garden. It should prove of value not only to gardeners but also to teachers setting up school wildlife areas and to conservation groups, especially urban ones, which are constantly being asked for help and advice.

With perhaps two million acres of gardens in Britain, the potential to bolster wildlife habitats and provide an important matrix of tiny nature reserves is obvious.

Since 1988, when this book first appeared in print, it has undergone several revisions and reprints so popular has it been, with over 22,000 copies sold. Now we have revised the text again and updated the references and supplier lists.

We have also added a preface about the need to garden in a sustainable way, encouraging you to have as little impact on the planet as you can. With the recent emphasis on quick garden makeovers, the need to be concerned about the environmental costs of gardening has become paramount.

These days there are many sources of help and advice. For example, local wildlife trusts have staff who can advise on wildlife gardening and there are many specialist leaflets and books dealing with all aspects of the subject.

Don't be daunted by the wealth of expertise around — we are all learning as we go! Whether you move towards wildlife gardening quickly or slowly, you will come to see what a rich and rewarding experience it can be. The first great spotted woodpecker coming to your peanut feeder or an egg-laying dragonfly at your pond will be moments to savour. This book should help you on your way.

Fran Hill

September 2000

# Contents

# *Plans and Charts*

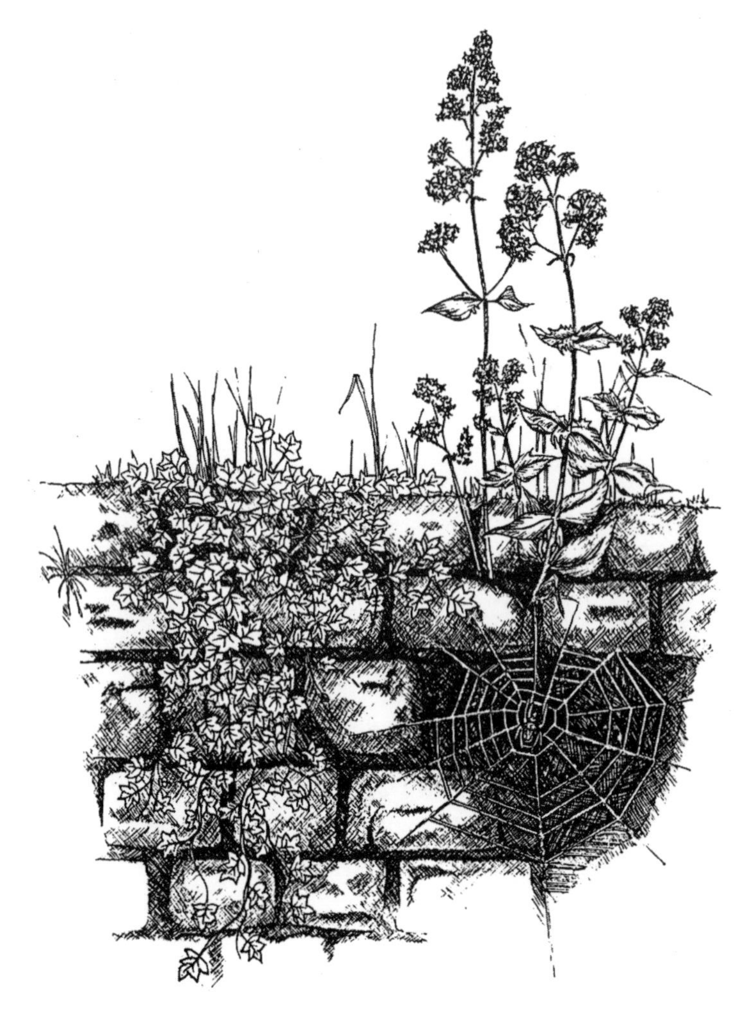

*Drystone wall with red valerian, ivy leaved toadflax and garden spider*
*by Daniel Rodrigues*

To Lorna, Laurie and Sam

# Before you start . . .

## . . . some guidelines

Even before you begin to design your wildlife garden please think carefully about the materials and methods you will use. The benefits of helping wildlife in your own garden will be pointless if your actions inadvertently contribute to the destruction of wild plants or animals or the habitats and countryside which they occupy.

Using sustainable materials and adopting organic methods is increasingly important as we try to reduce our impact on the planet. Here are some pointers to materials and methods to employ and those to avoid.

### Peat and compost

The use of peat by the garden industry is having a devastating effect on the rare plants and animals which are adapted to both our lowland and upland peat bogs.

In Britain, 80% of peat is extracted from three lowland sites, all of which are now designated as Sites of Special Scientific Interest (SSSIs). Unfortunately, before this protection was afforded, commercial extraction licences had been granted and these allow for their continued destruction.

Unless the demand for peat from gardeners reduces dramatically, the peat extraction companies will continue to destroy these very special habitats, both here and abroad. Organisations such as The Wildlife Trusts are campaigning against this destruction, so do join them and add your weight to their campaigns.

There are now many alternative, non-peat composts on the market. They require different techniques to get the best out of them. One example, coir, made from coconut husks, has met with much criticism from professional gardeners and indeed from those concerned about transporting this waste material from Asia and not making use of it locally.

Of course, the cheapest and probably most versatile alternative to peat is to make your own garden compost. It will save you money and it is very satisfying to create something from nothing! By recycling fruit and vegetable kitchen and garden waste, you will not only help to save peat bogs but also reduce the need for landfill sites.

The range of peat-free composts is being extended and improved all the time. If you need to buy compost be sure it is peat-free. You may have to experiment until you find one you like. Also, remember to let your garden centre know how you feel about them stocking peat and that there are now many peat-free alternatives.

### Gather no moss!

For years, moss has been used to line hanging baskets, for moss poles etc. As with peat, moss gathering from the wild causes ecological damage especially when it is taken in commercial quantities from nature reserves and wildlife sites. There are plenty of good alternatives to the use of moss so there really is no excuse for buying it. See page 53 for details.

### Gardening without chemicals

The aim of wildlife gardening is to create a series of healthy habitats supporting a wide variety of plants and animals. The use of chemicals to control pests will create an imbalance between organisms in the garden and is likely to kill beneficial creatures. It may also lead to a build-up of harmful residues in the soil and in the food chain.

For example, a slug weakened by eating a slug pellet may poison a frog or hedgehog which eats it, causing problems far beyond the target species.

It is quite possible to garden without the need for chemicals. While it is frustrating to lose plants to pests, it is better to tolerate some damage rather than knowingly causing greater damage to other wildlife.

There are many organic methods of gardening. They include companion planting and biological control. The latter involves either introducing specialist predators to do a particular job or encouraging local ones to thrive. These might be ladybirds and lacewings, which are excellent aphid eaters and which you can encourage by creating natural and artificial over-wintering sites.

Frogs are another example. Attracted by your garden pond, they will eat many potentially harmful creatures such as slugs, as will hedgehogs, song thrushes and toads.

Even though some slug pellets are reputed to be unpalatable or harmless to other wildlife, it is better to avoid them all together. There are many alternative methods such as hand picking, beer traps, biological control by the use of parasitic nematode worms and the application of deterrent materials (such as sharp sand) around vulnerable plants.

Try to avoid applying inorganic liquid or granular chemical feeds on your plants. This can lead to a build up of chemicals in the soil. Instead use organic, natural products such as bone meal, liquid feeds derived from seaweed and homemade foliar feeds, for example, by steeping comfrey leaves in water.

Avoid using herbicides and learn to be more tolerant of so-called weeds. Some, such as groundsel and herb robert, can be very valuable sources of seeds for birds like goldfinches and bullfinches.

Hand weeding, hoeing regularly round food crops and applying mulch to suppress weed growth are all appropriate methods of weed control. Of course, planting borders so tightly that there is no bare soil showing will prevent many weeds from getting established in the first place.

The Henry Doubleday Research Association, based at Ryton near Coventry, is one of the best sources of books, information and catalogues on organic gardening and is also well worth a visit (see page 67).

## Bonfires

Burning woody garden waste is the traditional way of getting rid of it. But this causes problems with neighbours as well as polluting the air. Local councils often have shredding schemes. Alternatively you can shred it yourself and then use the wood chip for paths or mulching. Treating the material as an asset and not as a problem is the best approach.

Building as many log and twig piles as you have room for is probably the best solution. They'll decay away slowly and provide valuable habitats as they rot.

## Water

Reducing water consumption is an important aspect of lessening our impact on the planet. Even in the UK, lowering of the water table due to abstraction caused wetlands and even rivers to dry up completely during the 1990s.

Gardens can use vast amounts of water so it is vital that we keep our usage as low as possible. Using rainwater collected from house and shed roofs reduces our demand for piped water. Being almost free of nutrients, you can also use it to top up ponds, thereby helping to control algae. If you can arrange for your bath and other 'grey' water to be available for the garden, that too reduces your demand for water.

## Using local, recycled materials

When selecting materials for paths, paving, garden boundaries and structures, try to use recycled or reclaimed products wherever possible. If they have a local origin, so much the better, saving the environmental costs of transport.

Use natural stone and gravel only if it is locally abundant. It is a sobering thought that the demand for water-weathered limestone by gardeners and landscape designers has led to the destruction of areas of limestone pavement (and other water worn limestone) which support rare and specialised plants and animals.

In addition, in some areas, the demand for garden stone has led to unscrupulous dealings in material stolen from old agricultural walls and buildings. You'll need to be on your guard!

If you insist on having a rock garden, why not make your own rocks (see page 52 for the recipe). These, once weathered, will look very natural.

For garden paths and steps, consider using recycled or reclaimed materials such as crushed or old (hard) bricks. Wood chip makes sense especially where paths are used infrequently.

Consider planting a hedge rather than erecting imported larch lap fencing. Hedges provide both privacy for you and a valuable, year-round wildlife habitat. Alternatively, use locally produced willow or hazel hurdles or buy trellises made from recycled timber.

Avoid using shingle or pebbles taken from beaches or hard wood timber cut from natural or ancient forests. Only timber from sustainably managed plantations should be used - look at the label to check.

Of course, if you can reclaim and use old timbers such as railway sleepers, so much the better. As a bonus, the use of these old or recycled materials will enhance the natural feel of your garden and will provide an ideal foil for your plants, as well as being kinder to the environment.

## Plant sources

To avoid negative impact on wildlife habitats, ensure that plants and bulbs you buy are from a reputable source. The commercial theft of bluebells, wild daffodils and other plants from the wild is a serious problem in some parts of the UK. It is also a very serious problem in places like Turkey, where the wholesale removal of wild cyclamen, anemones and other bulbs has brought many to the point of extinction.

Remember that it is illegal to dig up plants from the wild.

It is also important to use seeds, plants and trees of local provenance (origin) where possible (see the lists of reliable sources on pages 68-70). In addition, your wildlife trust may be able to advise you on local suppliers.

While the charts in this book list non-native trees, shrubs and plants which are good for wildlife, it is generally better to use species which grow in the wild locally. For example, if you were planting a new hedge, especially one adjoining countryside, using local hedging species would blend in far better than, say a single species hedge composed of a non-local species. What is 'local' will depend on where you live and may change within a matter of miles, so again, seek advice from your trust.

## Aliens

While many non-native plants exist happily within gardens, a few have escaped into the wild and have caused very serious problems. Rhododendron, himalayan balsam and japanese knotweed are three examples of plants which have spread from parks and gardens and have taken over huge areas of the countryside, so don't be tempted to plant them!

Similarly, there are many rampant, non-native water plants which cause havoc both in garden ponds and when released into the wild. These are described and listed on page 40.

Non-native animals such as bullfrogs and terrapins also threaten native species both in the garden and when they are accidentally or deliberately released into the countryside.

## Don't be deterred!

Having read all this, you may feel that the path to successful, low impact, wildlife gardening is paved with problems and difficulties. In reality, these are entirely manageable, taken one by one. Surmount them and you'll have earned a halo bright enough to attract a cloud of moths should you stumble out after dark to admire the results of your labours!

*Toad*

# CHAPTER 1

# Planning a Wildlife Garden

CREATING a garden from a new plot or an overgrown wilderness will allow you to design your ideal wildlife garden. However, many people have an established garden, part of which, perhaps, they may want to convert to help wildlife.

The thought of where to begin can be daunting. So start in a small way by planting a few wildflowers or a butterfly bush (buddleia) in the border, or put up a bird table and nest box and learn to be less fanatical about tidiness. You will probably be so fascinated by the results that you will have the enthusiasm to tackle more adventurous projects such as creating a pond, or completely restocking the herbaceous border with wild flowers.

Even a very formal garden can have small pockets of wildlife areas carefully included without making it look wild or uncontrolled. It is possible to retain formal areas around the house — but still create special wildlife habitats with informal or natural areas beyond.

However, do not fall into the trap of thinking that a wildlife garden will be maintenance free.

It will need managing but in a different way. So while adopting new attitudes to horticulture, read this book and decide what elements of wildlife gardening you would like to introduce into your plot.

The best way to begin designing any garden is to draw a scaled plan of the existing layout. First get some graph or tracing paper, a long tape and a friend to help do the measuring. Working to a plan will help to phase the work logically and deter you from jumping from project to project. The easiest way to do this is by triangulation (see Plan A). Plot the measurements on your graph paper using a suitable scale (you can use a rule but it is easier with a scale rule). I suggest 1:20 (i.e. 1 inch equals 20 inches or 1 cm equals 20 cms) for a tiny garden, 1:50 for a small to medium plot and 1: 100 for up to half an acre. Beyond this size it gets complicated and tedious using a tape measure.

Plot the fixed features in your garden that you want to retain — trees, shrubs, sheds, etc. Mark in the shade that they cast, also your house and fences. Indicate sunny/shady corners and the aspect of any walls or fences (i.e. south or east facing, etc.) Mark on hollows, slopes, changes of level, and test your soil (you can obtain a DIY soil testing kit from garden shops or centres). If you have had your garden for some years you will probably have got to know your soil and all the information above already.

The two plans illustrated on pages 7 and 8 give some ideas on how to design a wildlife garden. Plan B shows a small town garden and Plan C shows a medium/large garden. Chapter 6 includes an example of a paved wildlife garden. Try to include as many different elements as possible but without the garden becoming an incoherent jumble of features. Make sure everything is sited to look as natural as possible and planned to link harmoniously. Study the countryside and try to emulate it on a small scale. If you live in a rural area try and design your wildlife garden so that it flows into the surrounding countryside. For example, run your wildflower meadow up to an adjacent wood or field without an obvious boundary fence or hedge to create the illusion that the garden and countryside are one. If you need to define your boundaries plant hedges or build walls or fences in the local style or vernacular. Ensure you plant trees to frame but not block pleasant views — and conversely plant trees to block ugly views. You may have to reach a compromise where the trees are planned to function as a shelter belt; shelter versus view!

In an urban or suburban setting you can be more introspective in your design and create a small piece of countryside within your boundaries. However, take care not to aggravate neighbours by planting trees in a position which could eventually shade out the only sunny part of their garden. Remember too that trees and buildings in adjoining gardens will have localised effects on your plot.

Most importantly do remember that the best wildlife gardens are the ones which don't look too designed.

## Boundaries *(See chapters 2 and 6)*

Start by examining your boundaries — fences, hedges, walls (or lack of them). Think whether you could replace a sombre Leylandii hedge which robs the soil of all its goodness, or an ugly post and wire fence, with a delightful wild hedgerow full of colourful leaves, flowers and berries all year round. Why not cover a dull fence with berrying climbing shrubs or replace a privet hedge needing endless clipping with a formal but berrying hedge such as cotoneaster, pyracantha or sweet briar with its marvellous hips? Consider introducing native shrubs into an existing single species hedge, or plant some wildflowers in a drystone wall. There really are many things you can do to improve your outlook.

## Trees *(See Chapter 2)*

Have you got space to plant some trees? Every garden no matter how small should have at least one small tree if only to provide a songpost for the blackbird. If you have a large plot in an exposed position consider planting a small shelterbelt of windfirm native trees and shrubs, or plant a small copse in an awkward corner of your garden. If the trees start to get too big they can be coppiced or felled and others planted.

However, remember that trees will need room to expand and they will cast a lot of shade as they mature, so avoid siting them too near to buildings, ponds, your proposed sunny border or in positions where they may affect your neighbours.

## The Mixed Border *(See Chapter 3)*

Site a mixed border designed to provide food for nectar-loving insects such as bees and butterflies in a sunny sheltered part of the garden and in a position where you can sit and enjoy the sights and sounds of insects at work.

If your garden is small and lacking in sunshine it is still possible to create a valuable wildlife habitat by planting perennials and shrubs which will provide seeds, berries, nesting sites and plenty of cover. Try and select an area sheltered from cold winds. Avoid north and east facing parts of the garden where plants will be subjected to relatively cooler temperatures in summer and much harsher conditions in winter. Always choose an area where the soil is well drained.

## Flowery Meadows *(See Chapter 4)*

Part or all of your existing lawn can be converted into a flower-rich meadow. Any problem areas in the garden — places that are shady, excessively wet or dry where standard lawn grasses struggle — will be suitable for inclusion as wildflower areas.

Locate the meadow to form a link between other wildlife habitats, for example as a transition zone between mown lawn and hedge or between pond and woodland edge.

Ensure the meadow boundaries form bold curves. This is not only visually more pleasing but also makes mowing easier.

Regularly mown paths through the grasses and wild flowers will give access without the risk of trampling sensitive plants and animals.

## Siting a Pond *(See Chapter 5)*

A successful wildlife pond can become the focal point or highlight of a wildlife garden so it is vital to site it carefully.

A healthy pond needs to be in full sun for as many hours of the day as possible. It shouldn't be sited near drain pipes, cables or trees, for roots and shading can be problematical and rotting leaves in the water can cause stagnation unless regularly removed. You must allow for overspill — ideally into a planned marshy area or into a soakaway. It is also important that you don't issue excess water into your neighbour's garden, onto a highway or even into your house!

Ensure the chosen site is level or if your garden slopes, incorporate a rockery on the slope with a pond at its foot so it looks as natural as possible. Avoid siting the pond in an existing wet area — digging out soil will be extremely difficult and you will cause yourself all sorts of problems trying to keep a polythene or butyl liner from being pushed up by the water. Try and locate your pond so that various other elements in the garden abut it — perhaps a meadow area, gravel, rocks, or wet meadow. All of these will allow animals to crawl in and out easily if your pond has gently sloping edges. Some hard paving will allow you to enjoy pond dipping without the risk of slipping in!

## The Paved Garden *(See Chapter 6)*

You may decide to keep a formal area near the house with paving and seats. It is a good idea to plant scented wild flowers nearby and allow them to self-seed, to grow climbers up your walls and create planting areas within the paving. Plant up troughs, pots and hanging baskets with scented herbs and wildflowers, and plant low growing or creeping shrubs and perennials which will flop and spread to soften the harsh straight lines and colours of walls and paving.

Try to create many wildlife habitats both natural and artificial near the house by introducing dry-laid paving, gravel, a rockery, a small pond or drystone wall. Erect a bird table bird bath, nest box, a bat box and even a hedgehog house in a quiet corner. If you do these things, soon your former neat and sterile patio or terrace will become a charming place in which to relax and a very useful feeding and nesting site. The view from your kitchen or living room window will take on a new dimension.

## Paths *(See Chapter 6)*

In any garden, paths are necessary to allow you to walk around in comfort and without creating a quagmire or damaging vegetation.

To a certain extent you will be able to anticipate from your drawn plan where the more functional paths should go. But where paths are needed to enable you to wander around and enjoy your garden the route is more difficult to plot in theory. Generally it would be better to construct and plant the various elements in the garden and leave any path construction for a couple of seasons until desire lines become obvious. Only then surface your trampled routes with appropriate materials knowing that the paths are in the right place.

PLAN A

### Triangulation

Measure house — assume walls are at right angles. This gives you three points from which to triangulate. Measure from any two points you have fixed such as house corners A and B, A and C or B and C to any feature to be plotted.

**Example One** To plot the corner D of the garden, measure AD and CD. Set your compasses to the measurements required in scale and make two intersecting arcs to mark the position. If the boundary is not straight, plot several points along its length and draw a line through these to get the correct boundary shape.

**Example Two** To plot tree E measure AE and BE and draw on plan as above. Measure the tree spread. As a check measure EF from the trunk to the fence.

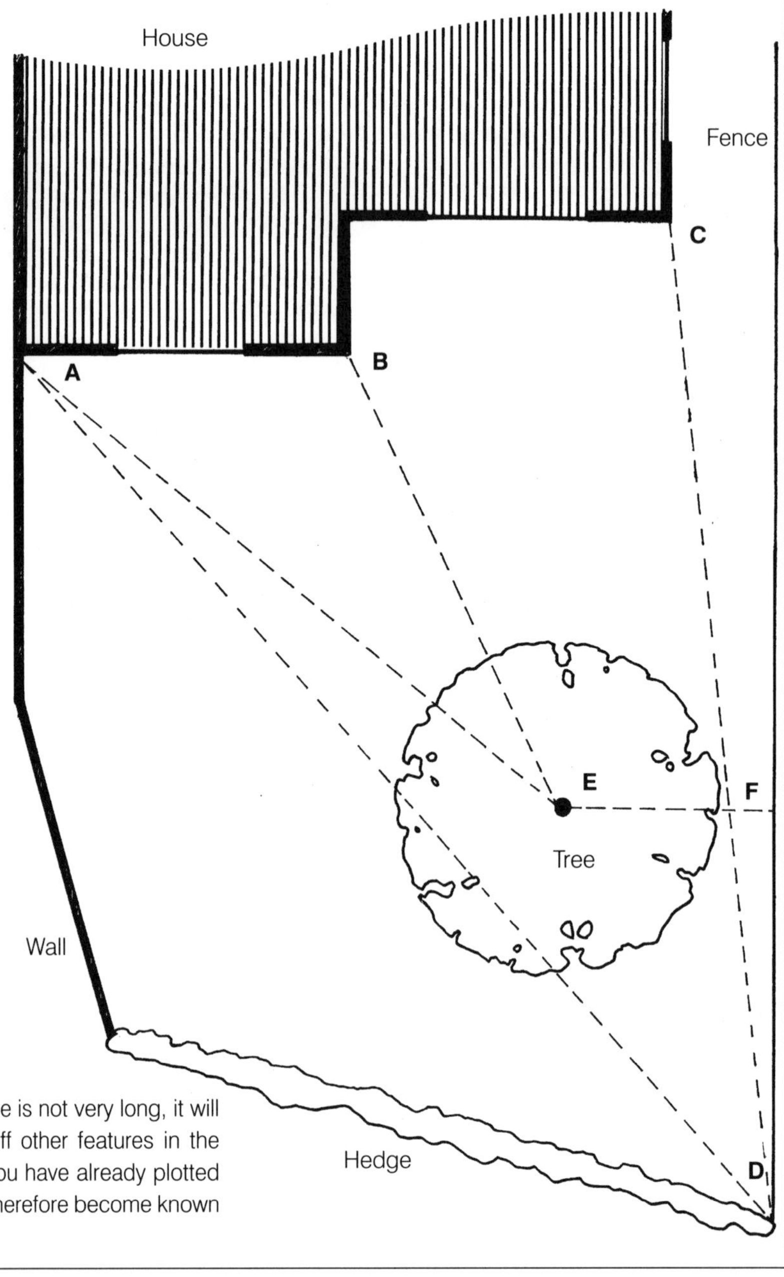


In a large garden or if your tape is not very long, it will be necessary to triangulate off other features in the garden such as trees which you have already plotted on your plan and which have therefore become known fixed points.

PLAN B

## Town Garden

**A** House with bat and tit boxes

**B** Ornamental hedge for berries and nectar (e.g. Cotoneaster)

**C** Mixed border: shrubs, garden flowers and wildflowers for butterflies

**D** Gravel garden with wildflowers growing through

**E** Dry-laid paving with wildflowers growing in joints and spaces

**F** Raised planting borders with drystone walls for herbs

**G** Climbing shrubs on trellis

**H** Bird table

**I** Pond planted with wetland wildflowers

**J** Gravel beach to allow animals to crawl in and out

**K** Pond liner extended to form marshy area

**L** Rockery planted with alpines and creeping wildflowers

**M** Berrying and seeding shrubs underplanted with ground cover plants

**N** Spring wildflower meadow — mown and used throughout summer

**O** Garage

**P** Timber pergola planted with climbers: hops, ivy, honeysuckle

**Q** Semi-shaded border for hedgerow wildflowers

**R** Greenhouse

**S** Compost bin

**T** Stack of logs to rot down

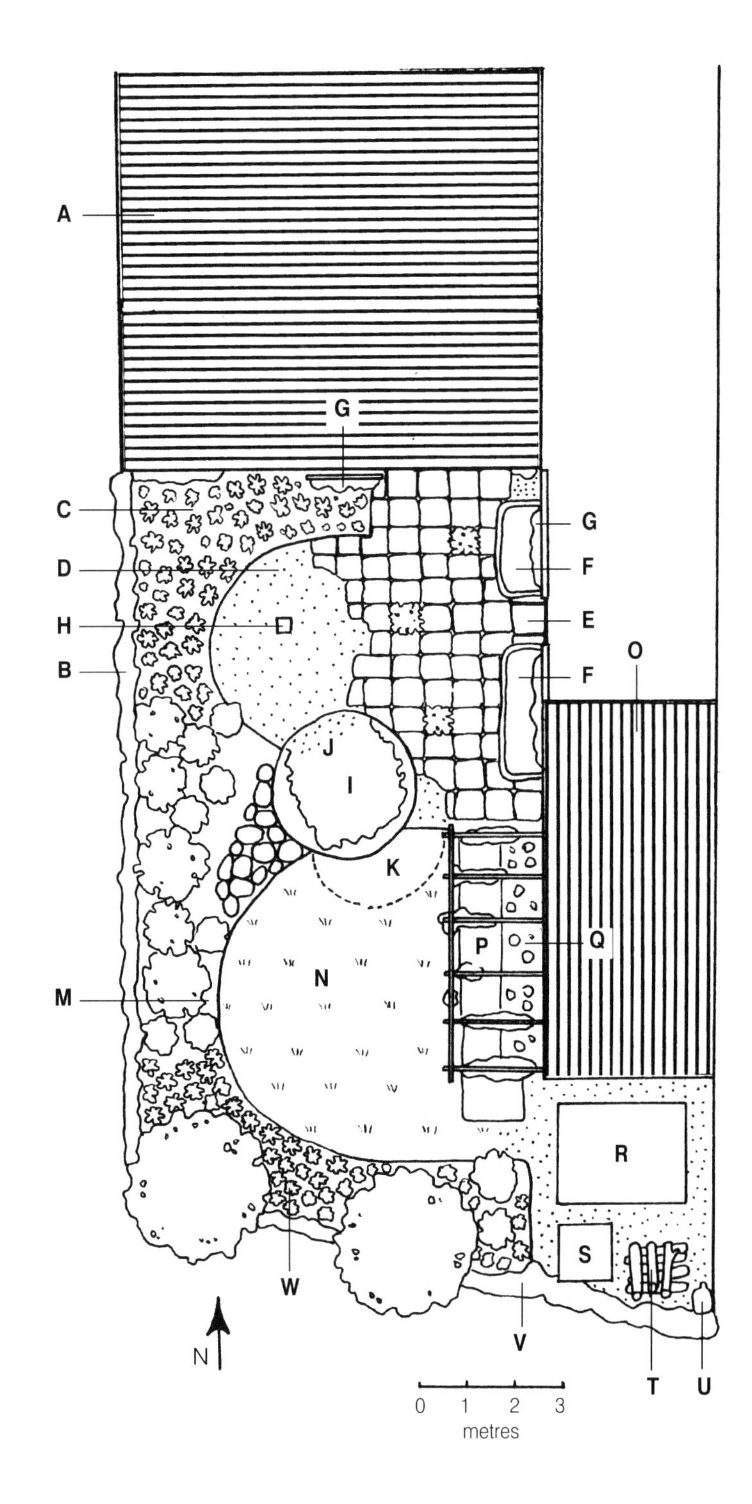


**U** Hedgehog house

**V** Mixed hedgerow with rowan and birch trees

**W** Hedgerow and woodland wildflower border

PLAN C

# Medium/Large Garden

**A** Birch and rowan trees in grass with naturalized bulbs

**B** Shrubbery and ground cover plants providing nectar, berries and shelter

**C** Mixed border — garden and wild shrubs and flowers

**D** Pond constructed with flexible liner

**E** Summer house with dry-laid stone paving
Wildflowers growing between slabs

**F** Cornfield wildflower border

**G** i Summer wildflower meadow

**G** ii Pond overspill —marshy spring meadow

**H** Shelter belt of native trees and shrubs

**I** Spring wildflower meadow

**J** Mixed hedgerow and hedgerow trees

**K** Regularly mown lawn

**L** Cottage garden plants in gravel garden

**M** Pyracantha hedge

**N** Sunken garden: Drystone retaining walls; climbing plants; wildflowers and herbs in troughs, pots and hanging baskets

**O** Vegetable garden

**P** Nursery bed for cultivating wildflowers

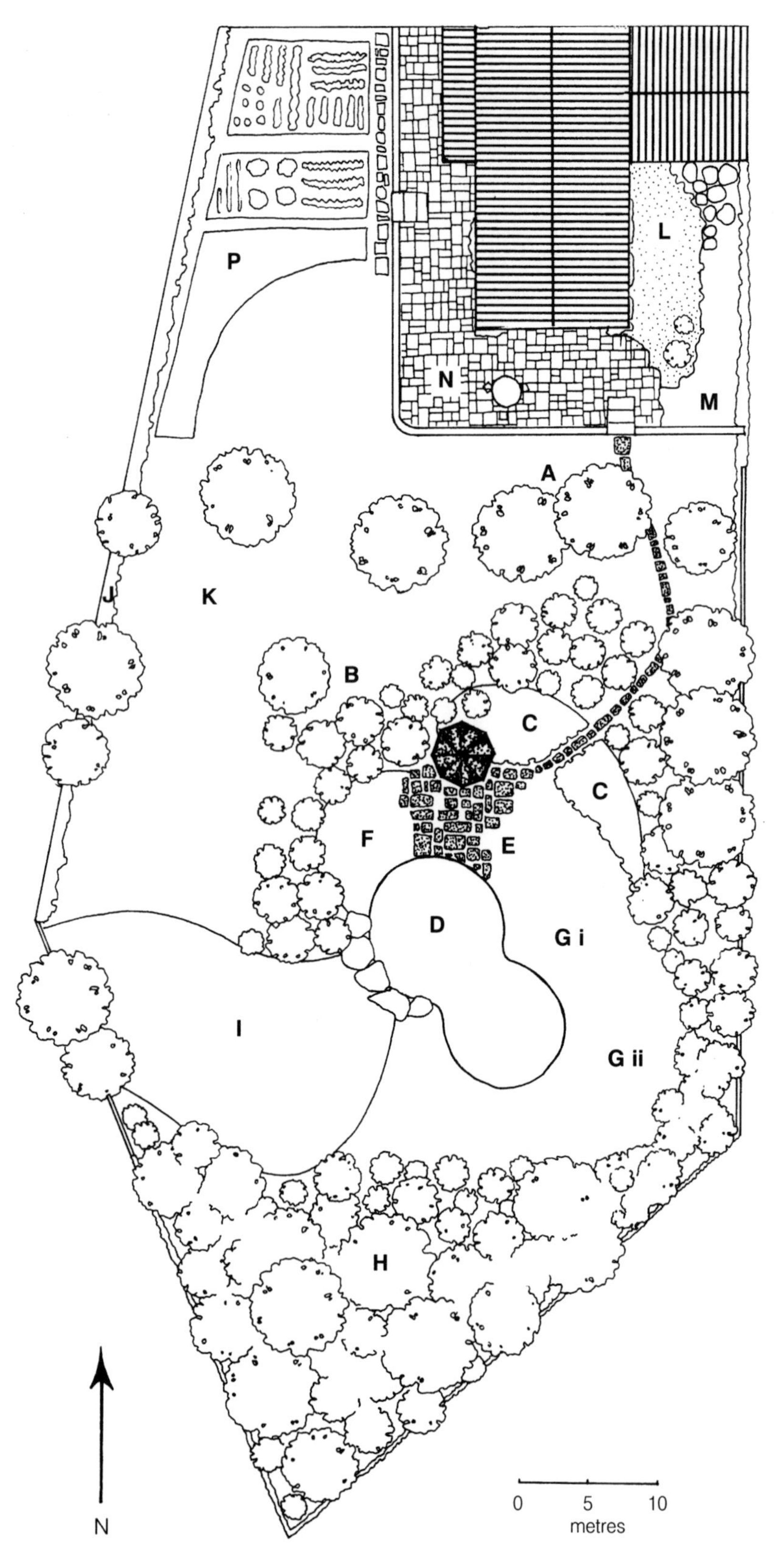

# CHAPTER 2

# Hedges and Trees

TREES and shrubs form the backbone of any garden whether it is designed for ornament or to attract wildlife. A garden comprised only of herbaceous plants, which die back in winter, will lack visual interest throughout the dormant months and likewise it will be devoid of shelter and food supplies for animals.

Trees and shrubs not only provide nesting, hibernation sites and food in the form of buds, berries and seeds but they are a vital breeding site for a huge number of insects and spiders which in turn are fed on by larger animals. Ornamental varieties support few, if any, insects so it is vital to plant native species. An added bonus for the wildlife gardener is that native varieties of trees and shrubs are cheaper to buy than their exotic counterparts. However, it is important to go to a reputable nursery to ensure the plants are truly native, and please, do not be tempted to dig up saplings from the wild.

*Deciduous woodland. Using native trees and shrubs is best if your garden is big enough*

## Hedges

Originally all lowland Britain was covered with mixed deciduous woodland, and this was gradually cleared to create agricultural land. Hedges that were planted to divide up the land provided an alternative habitat for wildlife that had previously existed in the woodland edge or in glades, i.e in conditions of dappled light cast by trees or in areas which are out of the sun for part of the day. Similar conditions can be created in the garden by planting a mixed hedge or border, a small spinney, or even a single clump of shrubs. By planting a mixed hedge a wide selection of shrubs, trees, climbers and wildflowers can be grown in a relatively small area. Even forest trees such as oak, ash and beech can be trimmed as part of the hedge and though not achieving their normal height will nonetheless provide valuable shelter, nesting and breeding sites for birds and insects.

### How to plant a mixed hedge

1. Preferably buy 'bare rooted', native trees and shrubs during the dormant months — both cheaper and more readily available than containerised ones. Aim to plant in the autumn when the soil is warm which aids root establishment. Planting can also be carried out during winter provided the ground is not frozen or waterlogged.

2. Select plants from Chart 1, pages 13-15. Aim for 70% hawthorn, 30% other shrubs and trees planted in groups but at random throughout the hedge. Choose plants to make the hedgerow colourful for as long a season as possible.

3. Prepare the ground to be planted. Dig it over carefully, removing all perennial weeds. Then dig a trench about 30-40 cms wide and fork plenty of well rotted manure, compost and leafmould, etc., into the bottom.

4. Water the trees and shrubs well before planting (ensure their roots are kept damp while they wait to be planted).

5. If there is sufficient space plant in two staggered rows, plants 30 cms apart, and rows 30-40 cms apart. This will give a good thick hedge. If you plant a single row of shrubs at forty-five degrees to the ground the new shoots will grow vertically to give a thick hedge bottom.

Alternatively, once planted, cut the shrubs and trees (to be pruned as shrubs) back to 15-20 cms to encourage bushy growth and aid root establishment. Spread the roots out well, backfill with soil/manure, firm well and water. Ensure soil level is not above the neck of the shrubs and trees, i.e. the line where the soil came to when they were in the ground.

6. Mulch the ground around the roots to preserve soil moisture and prevent weeds from choking young plants. Use grass clippings, old hay, chopped bark, special biodegradable matting or punctured black polythene (if you can stand its appearance!)

7. Cut the hedge hard for the first two seasons to encourage thick growth. Then let it grow up and trim annually until it reaches the required height and thickness. Once established aim to trim it annually in early winter to avoid bird nesting periods, wasting nuts and berries, and interfering with spring buds and growth. The best trimmed hedge shape is thicker at the bottom than the top. This prevents snow accumulating and splitting the hedge open.

8. If the hedge grows too thinly thicken it up by planting some extra shrubs.

9. Once the hedge gets established there is no longer need to mulch. Wild flowers will start to arrive as well as birds and small mammals such as mice, voles, hedgehogs and shrews hunting for insects, woodlice and spiders. Chart 2 lists some of the beautiful wildflowers which can be planted in the hedge bottom. See also Chart 5 on page 21.

Climbing shrubs and annual climbers can also be introduced, but avoid planting these when the hedge plants are still small or they will get swamped! Choose plants which flower in different seasons to ensure a nectar supply, seed source, and colour interest throughout the year. See Chart 17 on page 47.

10. If space permits plant some trees in the hedge or allow selected shoots from the hedge to grow up above the hedgeline. This will increase the supply of fruit, nuts, and nectar and also create three layers of vegetation — each layer favoured by certain birds. The low vegetation and leaf litter will attract dunnocks,

*Hedgerow bottom with woodmouse, snails, primroses and wild arum*

blackbirds and wrens (as well as amphibians and small mammals). Finches and robins enjoy the intermediate shrub layer, and mistle thrushes and tits prefer the tree tops.

11. The best wildlife hedge is one which is allowed to grow semi-wild so that trees and shrubs flower and fruit to provide a wildlife food source. However, this can take up a lot of space, which is not practical in most gardens. Such a loose hedge is not always best for nest building.

12. If space is really restricted, or there are already good boundary fences — create a type of hedge by training ornamental and native shrubs and climbers against the panels. Dig a narrow border along the base to plant with partial shade loving wildflowers.

*Guelder rose*

13. A single species hedge of ornamental or native shrubs can make good nesting sites and if selected carefully can be a valuable nectar and berry resource. See Chart 4, page 18.

# Trees

Native trees are an important feature in the wildlife garden. They provide shelter from wind, shade, nesting sites, food, song perches and roosting sites and are host to a huge number of invertebrates and their larvae.

Larger trees are suitable only for gardens of half an acre or more, although in a smaller garden they can be coppiced, i.e cut back hard every few years so that new shoots grow from the base, or they can be grown as shrubs in the hedge. Chart 1 shows which trees and shrubs are suitable for a range of garden sizes.

## Buying and planting trees

1. Buy from a reputable nursery to ensure the trees are truly native.

2. Trees are sold as whips, feathered, half standard, standard, heavy standard or semi-mature. Generally ignore the last two categories. Whips are small, cheap and useful if a large area is to be planted. They may need to be protected with rabbit guards. Small feathered trees are comparatively cheap and a good buy. They are still fairly economical for mass planting and give a good effect. Half standards and standards are good for specimen trees but need to be staked and are slower to establish.

3. As with hedging plants, it is cheapest to buy bare rooted trees and best to plant between October to March.

4. Check the tree has a good root ball which has not been allowed to dry out or been damaged. If you buy well in advance of planting, water the roots thoroughly and heel them in, i.e. dig a trench and temporarily plant the trees with their roots covered with soil.

5. Check the leading shoot is healthy (you often find it has been damaged, and cut off for another shoot to take the lead).

6. Check buds for signs of disease or mildew.

7. If you want to plant larger trees try to select good straight specimens. An economic size to buy is 1.5-2m. tall, feathered or standard. Larger trees are comparatively far more expensive and are more likely to fail. Often growth is checked in transplanting more so than with smaller trees.

*Siskin on alder*

## How to plant a tree

1. Thoroughly soak tree roots.

2. Dig a hole big enough to allow enough room for roots and dig in some well rotted manure or compost.

3. Drive stake in firmly on the windward side.

4. Plant tree, spreading out the roots. Infill with soil, ensuring it does not come above the previous soil line on the stem. Firm in well and then water.

5. Secure tree to stake with tree tie. Use a short stake and one tie to allow the crown to move about in the wind which in turn promotes root development.

6. Check trees regularly subsequently making sure they don't work loose or dry out. Check the tie is not too tight.

7. Remove stake after two years.

### Planting a copse or group of trees

1. Prepare ground well (as for hedges).

2. Plant in groups of three to five (depending on area to be planted), trees 1-1.5m. apart. This will encourage growth and the leaf cover will exclude light and help to suppress rampant weeds.

3. Select trees of varying eventual heights (if they grow too tall they can be coppiced or thinned out) and include some native shrubs so that a three or four layered effect is eventually achieved, i.e. taller trees, coppiced or small trees, shrubs, and ground flora. A layered effect will attract the greatest variety of wildlife.

4. Stake trees if site is exposed or standards are planted. In a rural area where rabbits may be a problem, fit tree guards.

5. Mulching with organic matter for the first few years will help tree and shrub growth by providing nutrients, conserving water and suppressing weeds. Chopped bark is especially good. It is a bit expensive but well worth the money as it will discourage weeds more effectively than leafmould or compost. Chopped bark is a habitat in itself for invertebrates, fungi and bacteria as it starts to rot down. Mixed with fallen leaves a natural woodland floor will start to develop.

6. After several years the trees can be thinned — selecting the best trees to grow on and felling or coppicing others. Pile up some logs, leaves and branches in the mini-woodland to provide a habitat for invertebrates.

7. In a small garden where access is needed below and between trees it is a good idea to prune off the lower branches each year using sharp secateurs to form a clear trunk of 1.2-1.5m. or so. Prune in the dormant months October to March.

8. If two leading shoots develop on a young tree prune the weakest one to encourage the other to grow straight. If you have a large area of trees you don't have to be so purist about this.

9. Once the trees are really getting established allow the mulch to rot down and wild seeds will start to germinate in the spinney. Plant hedgerow or semi-shade loving wildflowers along the woodland edge, or create a sunny clearing in the trees to grow these. Plant shade tolerant species amongst the trees and shrubs. Plant in bold groups and the wildflowers and spring bulbs will gradually seed and spread to find their preferred conditions.

*Charts 2 and 3 will help you select appropriate plants for the soil and conditions involved.*

CHART 1

# Trees and shrubs for the wildlife garden

*Note: A cross indicates suitability — i.e. Alder will grow in shade, does tolerate coppicing, etc.*
**Indicates large trees which should only be grown in gardens of more than half an acre*

| | Soil preference | Approx. height at maturity | Growth rate | Shade | Can withstand Exposure | Coppicing (cutting back) | Suitable for mixed hedge | Suitable for small/med. garden | Wildlife notes |
|---|---|---|---|---|---|---|---|---|---|
| **Alder*** *Alnus glutinosa* | Damp, most | (60') 18m | Moderate | X | | X | | X if coppiced | Seeds popular with siskins and other birds. Good tree for poorly drained parts of the garden. |
| **Alder Buckthorn** *Frangula alnus* | Damp acid esp. peat | (8') 2.5m | Moderate | | | | X | | Berries for birds. Few insects attracted but important food plant for brimstone butterfly larvae |
| **Ash*** *Fraxinus excelsior* | Most | (70') 21m | Fast | | X | X | | | Keys eaten by small mammals and birds. Few insects associated with it. |
| **Aspen*** *Populus tremula* | Wet heavy clays | (80') 24m | Fast | X | X | X | | | Fair insect fauna. |
| **Beech*** *Fagus sylvatica* | Dry well drained | (90') 27m | Slow | X | X | X | X | | Casts dense shade so poor ground flora. Fair number of insects. Seeds (mast) for small mammals and many birds. |
| **Birch*** *Betula pendula* | Most - dry acid best | (60') 18m | Fast | X | X | X | | X | Small leaves — good ground flora. Excellent for insects and to attract insect-eating birds. Best tree for moth larvae. Catkins good food source for birds. Casts light shade. |
| **Bird Cherry** *Prunus padus* | Most fertile esp. alkaline | (20') 6m | Moderate | | | | | X | Flowers attractive to insects. Berries for birds and small mammals. |
| **Blackthorn** *Prunus spinosa* | Most fertile | | Fast | | X | | X | X | Good for nesting birds if grown as thicket or in hedge. Rich in insects. Berries for birds. (excellent for sloe gin!) |
| **Buckthorn** *Rhamnus catharticus* | Damp calcareous | (15') 4.5m | Moderate | | | | | X | Host plant for brimstone butterfly caterpillar. |
| **Crab Apple** *Malus sylvestris* | Most fertile | (30') 9m | Moderate | | | | X | X | Fruit eaten by birds and small mammals. Many insect species associated with tree. |
| **Dogrose** *Rosa canina* | Most fertile not wet | Rambling | Moderate | | | | X | X | Hips good food source for birds and small mammals. Excellent grown through hedge — good nesting. |
| **Elderberry** *Sambucus nigra* | Most fertile | (33') 10m | Fast | | X | | X | X | Few insect larvae. Nectar and berries. Good nest site. Good for wine! |

| | *Soil preference* | *Approx. height at maturity* | *Growth rate* | *Shade* | *Can withstand Exposure* | *Coppicing (cutting back)* | *Suitable for mixed hedge* | *Suitable for small/med. garden* | *Wildlife notes* |
|---|---|---|---|---|---|---|---|---|---|
| **Wild Cherry** *Prunus avium* | Good soil pref. alkaline | (50') 20m | Fast | | | | | X | Fruits eaten by a variety of birds. Few insects. |
| **Gorse** *Ulex europaeus* | Dry, poor acid | (8') 2.4m | Slow | | X | | | X | Moderate insect fauna. Good for nesting birds. |
| **Guelder Rose** *Viburnum opulus* | Most, damp | | Moderate | X | X | | X | X | Nectar for insects, particularly hoverflies. Fruits for birds and small mammals, especially liked by woodmouse. |
| **Goat Willow** *Salix caprea* | Damp fertile loams | (30') 9m | Rapid | | X | X | X | X | Very rich insect fauna. Early catkins for insects. |
| **Hawthorn** *Crataegus monogyna* | Most | (20') 6m | Moderate | X | X | X | X | X | Nectar. Hips good food source for thrushes, etc. Good nesting if dense. Excellent for moth larvae. |
| **Hazel** *Corylus avellana* | Most | (20') 6m | Slow | X | X | X | X | X | Hazel nuts good food source for birds and small mammals |
| **Holly** *Ilex aquifolium* | Well drained | (50') 15m | Slow | X | X | X | X | X | Fruit popular with thrushes. Dense foliage gives good early nesting sites. Host to holly blue butterfly. Only female trees produce berries. |
| **Hornbeam*** *Carpinus betulus* | Heavy neutral to acid | (70') 21m | Slow | X | X | X | X | | Useful nesting cover if grown 2m high x 60cms thick. Seeds for birds |
| * **Lime (small leaved)** *Tilia cordata* | Heavy neutral (fertile) to acid | (60') 18m | Moderate | X | X | X | | | Few invertebrates feed on leaves. Flowers attract insects, particularly bees. Useful nesting cover. |
| **Maple (Field or Common)** *Acer campestre* | Clay or loam | (50') 15m | Moderate | X | | X | X | X | Fruits eaten by small mammals. Flowers attractive to insects. Few invertebrates feed on leaves. |
| **Oak (Pedunculate)*** *Quercus robur* | Heavy soils | (100') 30m | Slow | | X | X | X | | Acorns — food for birds, small mammals and insects. Most important trees for wildlife. |
| **Oak (Sessile)*** *Quercus petraea* | Light soils | (100') 30m | Slow | | X | X | X | | Excellent as food plant for insects, particularly moths — very important for insect-eating birds. |
| **Rowan** *Sorbus aucuparia* | Most soils | (30') 9m | Moderate | | X | | | X | Fair insect fauna. Flowers attract insects (nectar) Fruits eaten by birds, especially thrushes. No nests. Casts light shade. |
| **Scots Pine*** Pinus sylvestris | Dry sandy soils | (80') 27m | Fast | | X | | | | Good variety of insects feed on pine. Best conifer for wildlife. |

| | Soil preference | Approx. height at maturity | Growth rate | Shade | Can withstand Exposure | Coppicing (cutting back) | Suitable for mixed hedge | Suitable for small/med. garden | Wildlife notes |
|---|---|---|---|---|---|---|---|---|---|
| **Spindle** *Euonymus europaeus* | Alkaline | (20') 6m | Vigorous | | | | | X | Nectar for insects. Fruit for birds. |
| **Sweet Briar** *Rosa rubiginosa* | Most fertile | (3-10') 1-3m | Moderate | | | | X | X | Hips food source for small mammals and birds. Good nesting cover. |
| **Sallow** *Salix cinerea* | Damp fertile loams | (30') 9m | Fast | | X | X | X | X | Rich insect fauna |
| **Wild Privet** *Ligustrum vulgare* | Most esp. alkaline | (5') 1.50m | Fast | X | | | X | X | Birds feed on fruit, nest in dense tangles. Flowers attract insects. |
| **Wayfaring Tree** *Viburnum lantana* | Most esp. alkaline | (10') 3m | Moderate | | X | | | X | Berries food for birds. Flowers attract insects. |
| **Wild Service Tree*** *Sorbus torminalis* | Clay soil | (80') 25m | Moderate | | | | | | Nectar. Fruits eaten by birds. |
| **Whitebeam** *Sorbus aria* | Most pref. alkaline | (35') 15m | Moderate | | X | | | X | Relatively poor insect fauna. Flowers attract insects. Fruit eaten by birds. |

## Plants for butterfly caterpillars

Apart from the whites, our other butterflies (and indeed many moths and other insects) will only breed in gardens if the correct larval food plants are provided. This is an important step beyond having your garden function merely as a feeding station for adults.

Butterflies are usually quite specific about which plants they will lay their eggs on. Everyone knows that cabbage whites lay theirs on cabbages, other brassicas and even on nasturtiums, often causing serious damage. Checking for eggs or caterpillars and removing them by hand is effective if tedious.

**List of larval food plants and their associated butterflies:**

**Nettles** for small tortoiseshells, red admirals, peacocks and comma's. Note that the female butterflies select young nettles growing in sunny locations. For best results cut your nettle patches two or three times each summer, checking for eggs/caterpillars first of course!

**Jack by the Hedge and Lady's Smock:** for orange tips and green veined whites.

**Purging and Alder Buckthorn:** for brimstones.

**Birds foot trefoil:** for common blues.

**Holly and Ivy:** for holly blues.

**A range of grasses:** for meadow browns, gatekeepers, speckled woods and small and large skippers.

**Sorrel and Dock:** for small coppers.

**Creeping Thistle:** for painted ladies. However, thistles are 'noxious weeds' and it is illegal to allow them to grow and especially to seed. This also applies to ragwort, the food plant for the cinnabar moth, which is poisonous to horses and cattle. To be safe, don't allow either plant to grow in your garden. If you discover them mid-season, be sure they don't set seed! In waste places and in many uncultivated fields, both these plants thrive and are common. Best to let painted ladies and cinnabar moths breed there.

*Orange tip butterfly on lady's smock*

CHART 2

## Woodland wildflowers to grow in shade

| | Flowering period | Soil preference | Height (cms) | Aspect S (sun) Sh (shade) Ps (partial shade) | Annual (A) Biennial (B) Perennial (P) |
|---|---|---|---|---|---|
| **Woodruff** *Galium odoratum (White)* | May-June | Rich alkaline pref. | 15-30 | Sh/Ps | P |
| **Green Hellebore** *Helleborus viridis (Green)* | Feb-Mar | Most fertile | 45 | Sh/Ps | P |
| **Lungwort** *Pulmonaria officinalis (Blue/pink)* | Mar-May | Fertile moist | 30 | Sh/Ps | P |
| **Ramsons** *Allium ursinum (White)* | Apr-June | Fertile moist | 30-45 | Sh/Ps | P |
| **Water Avens** *Geum rivale (Purple/pink)* | May-Sept | Wet most | 45-60 | Sh/S/Ps | P |
| **Wood Avens** *Geum urbanum (Yellow)* | June-Aug | Fertile | 30-60 | Sh/Ps | P |
| **Wild Angelica** *Angelica sylvestris (White/pale pink)* | July-Aug | Fertile moist | 30-150 | Sh/S/Ps | P |
| **Wood Sorrel** *Oxalis acetosella (Pink)* | Apr-May | Most | 5-10 | Sh/Ps | P |
| **Wood Spurge** *Euphorbia amygdaloides (Lime green)* | Apr-May | Moist not acid | 30-80 | Sh/Ps | P |
| **Oxlip** *Primula elatior (Yellow)* | May | Most moist | 30 | Sh/S/Ps | P |
| **Sweet Violet** *Viola odorata (Purple)* | Feb-Apr | Fertile moist | 10-15 | Sh/Ps | P |

*See also Chart 5, page 21, for details of:*
Lily of the Valley, Snowdrop, Wood Anemone, Primrose, Wild Daffodil, Bluebell, Nettle Leaved Bellflower, Bugle, Sheep's Bit Scabious, Red Campion, Betony, Hedge Woundwort, Wood Cranesbill, Aquilegia.

*See Chart 8, page 25, for ground cover plants, Chart 3, page 17, for hedgerow wildflowers and for ferns see Chart 10, page 26.*

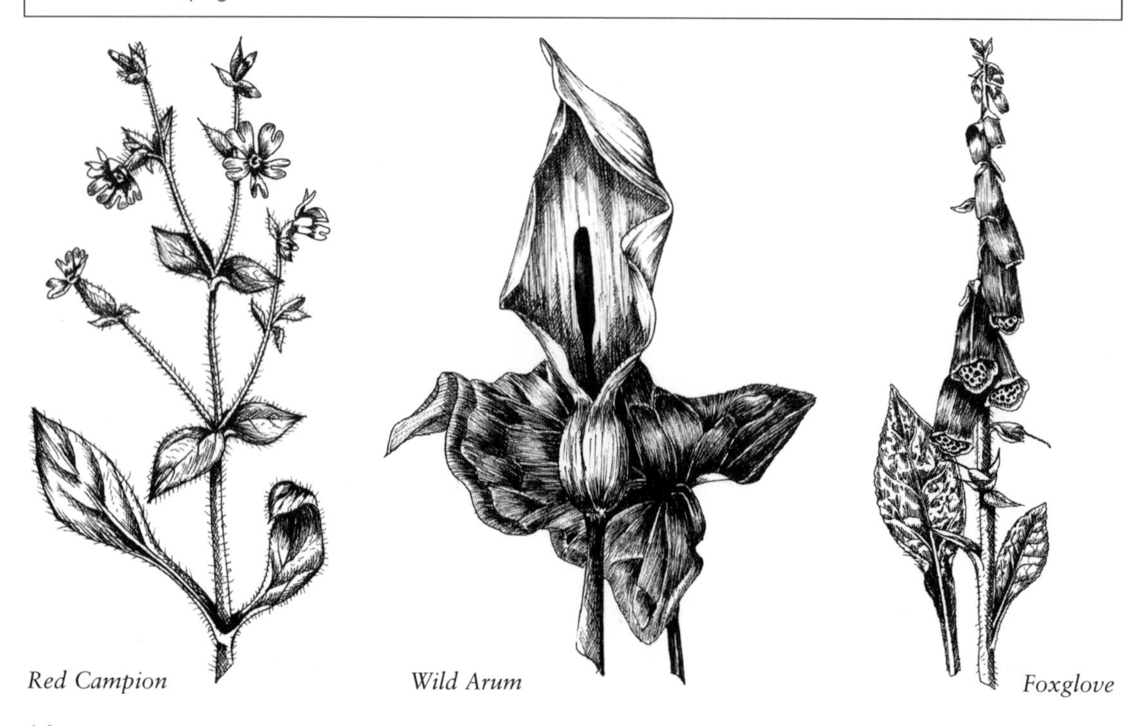

*Red Campion* *Wild Arum* *Foxglove*

CHART 3

## Hedgerow wildflowers to grow in partial light or dappled shade

| | Flowering period | Soil preference | Height (cms) | Aspect S (sun) Sh (shade) Ps (partial shade) | Annual (A) Biennial (B) Perennial (P) |
|---|---|---|---|---|---|
| **Yellow Archangel** *Lamiastrum galeobdolon (Yellow)* | May-June | Most damp pref. | 20-60 | Sh/Ps | P |
| **Wild Arum** *Arum maculatum (Green)* | Apr-June | Fertile | 30-50 | S/SH/Ps | P |
| **Herb Robert** *Geranium robertianum (Pink)* | Apr-Sept | Most esp. acid | 10-40 | S/Sh/Ps | A |
| **Greater Stitchwort** *Stellaria holostea (White)* | Apr-June | Fertile moist | 15-60 | S/Ps | P |
| **Common Dog Violet** *Viola riviniana (Purple/blue)* | Mar-May | Most | 2-10 | S/Ps | P |
| **Perforate St. John's Wort** *Hypericum perforatum (Yellow)* | June-Sept | Most | 30-90 | S/Ps | P |
| **Tufted Vetch** *Vicia cracca (Purple)* | July-Sept | Most | 60-100 | S/Ps | P |
| **Hedge Bedstraw** *Galium mollugo (White)* | June-Sept | Well drained | 45-100 | S/Ps | P |
| **Ground Ivy** *Glechoma hederacea (Mauve)* | Mar-May | Fertile moist | 10-30 | S/Sh/Ps | P |
| **White Deadnettle** *Lamium album (White)* | May-Dec | Most fertile | 20-60 | S/Ps | P |
| **Lesser Celandine** *Ranunculus ficaria (Yellow)* | Mar-May | Moist neutral | 8-20 | S/Ps/Sh | P |
| **Sweet Cicely** *Myrrhis odorata (White)* | May-June | Most | 60-90 | S/Ps | P |
| **Rough Chervil** *Chaerophyllum temulentum (White)* | June-July | Fertile | 30-90 | S/Ps | B |
| **Germander Speedwell** *Veronica chamaedrys (Blue)* | Mar-June | Most | Creeping | S/Ps | P |

(1) *See also Chart 5, pages 21-22, for details of:*

Bugle, Wild Strawberry, Solomon's Seal, Wood Anemone, Primrose, Wild Daffodil, Bluebell, Nettle Leaved Bellflower, Devil's Bit Scabious, Hedgerow Cranesbill, Betony, Hedge Woundwort, Red Campion, Foxglove.

(2) *All woodland wildflowers in Chart 2, page 16.*

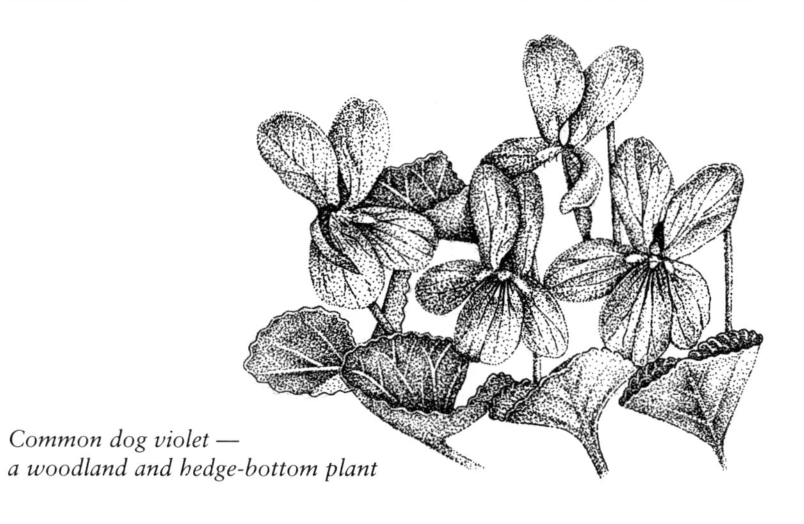

*Common dog violet — a woodland and hedge-bottom plant*

CHART 4

# Single species hedges to benefit wildlife

## Formal Hedges – while not often used in wildlife gardens, they can have some benefits

| | |
|---|---|
| **Hornbeam**<br>*Carpinus betulus* | Forms dense windbreak or screen, retains brown leaves through winter. Catkins appear in late spring — if hedge is left unclipped winged nutlets follow. Prefers sun or light shade. Plant hornbeams 45 cms apart. Trim annually early autumn (after nutlets have been eaten). Height 1.5-2.5m. after six years.<br>If grown to 2 m. high and 60 cms thick, good for nesting birds. |
| **Beech**<br>*Fagus sylvatica* | Pollen for bees. Nesting sites for blackbird, thrush, hedge sparrow, and finches. Deciduous, retains brown foliage all winter. Grows well in most soils except wet, heavy — good on chalk. Prefers sun or light shade. Plant 45 cms apart — cut off top quarter after planting — trim annually, late summer. Slow to establish. 1.2 m. after six years. Grow to 2 m. high by 60 cms thick for nesting birds. |
| **Holly**<br>*Ilex aquifolium* | Berries for birds, nectar for bees. Nesting sites.<br>Evergreen prickly hedge. Red berries in autumn and winter if male tree nearby. Grows in sun or part shade. Plant 60 cms apart. Trim in autumn/winter after berries eaten. Height 1.2 m. after six years. |
| **Yew**<br>*Taxus baccata* | Slow, berry-bearing evergreen hedge. Hardy and tolerant of most soils and conditions. Plant 60 cms apart. Pinch out leading shoots to encourage dense growth. Height 1 m. after six years. Useful for nesting if lightly clipped and grown to 2 m. |

## Informal Hedges

| | |
|---|---|
| **Berberis**<br>*Berberis stenophylla —*<br>*Berberis darwinii* | Berries for birds, nectar for bees. Grow to 1.5 m. high, well clipped, for nesting blackbird, thrush, hedge sparrow, greenfinch, linnet.<br>Forms wide evergreen hedge (1.8 m. wide). Golden flowers in spring, berries in autumn. Grows in sun or light shade. Plant 50 cms apart, 1. 8-2.5 m. after six years. |
| **Firethorn**<br>*Pyracantha rogersiana* | Nectar for bees, berries for birds.<br>Evergreen. Avoid heavy clipping or will not form berries. Plant 60 cms apart. Height 1.8-2.5m. after four years. |
| **Cotoneaster**<br>*Cotoneaster simonsii* | Berries for birds, nectar for bees. Nesting sites only if grown against a wall.<br>Erect semi-evergreen with colourful leaves and berries. Plant 45 cms apart. Trim in winter. Height 1.5-1.8m. ultimately. |
| **Privet**<br>*Ligustrum vulgare* | Berries for birds, nectar for butterflies. If open grown good for nests.<br>Semi-evergreen. White flowers in summer. Do not clip regularly — allow berries to develop. Plant 45 cms apart. Fast growing 1.2-1.8m. after three years. |
| **Hawthorn**<br>*Crataegeus monogyna* | Thick and thorny. Blossom in spring and berries in autumn. |
| **Blackthorn**<br>*Prunus spinosa* | Very spiny. White blossom in spring. Sloes in autumn. |

CHAPTER 3

# The Mixed Border

IN many gardens the traditional herbaceous border has been replaced with the mixed border. Although the herbaceous border is often a spectacular sight in the summer months, for the rest of the year it is uninteresting yet needs considerable maintenance.

By including ferns, annuals, perennials, shrubs and even small trees, the well planned mixed border can be of interest throughout the year.

*Jacob's ladder*

By planting native wildflowers and shrubs alongside ornamental varieties selected for their value to wildlife as nectar, seed and berry producers and as breeding sites for insects, you can create a beautiful border which is also a valuable wildlife habitat. Once established it will provide food, shelter and nesting sites for a whole host of insects, notably butterflies and bees, birds and small mammals.

## Guidelines to planting your mixed border

1. Aim to create a three layered effect, with taller shrubs and small trees as the top layer, a middle layer of medium sized perennials, annuals and shrubs, with a ground layer of bulbs, ferns, ground hugging or creeping shrubs and plants.

2. Start off by planting the border in the conventional way, i.e. small plants at the front, graded in height towards the back of the border, but as plants self-seed and newcomers establish themselves the border will take on a more natural appearance as plants find their preferred positions.

3. When designing an ornamental border it is general practice to grow flowers of similar or complimentary colours in the same area or the effect can be gawdy and unrestful. However, this rule does not apply where wildflower gardening is concerned. The flowerheads of wild plants are more subtle and contrasting colours exist quite happily side by side. When mixing wild and ornamental plants experiment with simple colour themes — 'hot' borders of yellows, reds, oranges; 'cool' borders of blue, mauve, white; or a 'restful' border of pastel shades.

4. Try and ensure continuity of flowering from early spring to autumn for nectar seeking insects, and choose berrying shrubs and trees to provide a winter food source for birds and small mammals. Include evergreen varieties to provide winter cover and shelter. Leave seed heads on annuals and perennials for finches to enjoy.

5. Choose old fashioned cottage garden flowers and herbs to accompany your wildflowers. Many modern ornamental flowers have been selectively bred for brightness of colour, size of flower — often double, which has in many cases resulted in flower sterility, i.e. no seeds or nectar will be produced, making them useless for wildlife. Old fashioned flowers and herbs are usually single-flowered and more like their wild relatives and hence are of more value in the wildlife garden. Wildflowers and insects have evolved together and are interdependent. It is important in the wildlife garden to provide not only food, but also breeding sites. Many insects will lay their eggs on a very limited range or often only on a single species.

6. Aim to plant densely leaving no bare soil. The spaces between permanent shrub and perennial planting can be filled with quick growing annuals.

7. Select plants not only for flower colour but form, colour and texture of their leaves.

8. If shrubs grow too large prune them carefully but avoid the nesting season and allow berries to ripen, i.e. avoid pruning after flowering.

9. Plant wildflowers from seed (see Chapter 8), or buy plants or plantlets from recognised nurseries (see list of suppliers at end of book).

*Devil's bit scabious* *Dame's violet*

10. Start by planting your wildflowers and shrubs in their preferred conditions of soil, sun, shade and moisture. As they self-seed and these seeds germinate you may be surprised to find shade loving plants thriving in the sun, and vice-versa.

11. When you have sown seed directly into the ground you may want to thin the seedlings or transplant some. Thinning is not essential as in nature the strongest seedlings will thrive at the expense of the weak ones.

12. Because wildflowers often have more subtle flower heads plant them en masse for greatest effect.

13. Plant seeds over a period of time and dead head them to increase their flowering period. Leave some to go to seed.

14. Avoid using fertilisers — good garden soil will encourage healthy growth. In fact many wildflowers will grow larger than they generally do in the wild. If growth is too lush this may attract pest problems.

15. Garden organically and avoid using pesticides. By growing a wide variety of plants you will attract many natural predators into your garden which will control any potential pests. Even one use of a spray could upset the balance of predators to prey and could aggravate the pest problem.

16. Wildflower gardening will enable you to plant up what could be problem areas in a conventional garden — dry poor soil, waterlogged or shady areas. There are many wildflowers adapted to such conditions.

17. A sunny position is best for planting a border to attract butterflies and bees. Butterflies particularly will be encouraged to visit your garden if you provide a suntrap, i.e. a border in a sheltered south facing corner protected by a wall or fence planted with nectar-rich flowers — an ideal position in which to site your garden chair!

18. Weed your border selectively. Learn to recognise seedlings of plants that are desirable and those such as dock, creeping thistle, buttercup, field bindweed, couch grass and ground elder, which are not. The secret to wildflower gardening is to let nature partly take over your designed border letting plants pop up all over the place. But nature can't be left to her own devices or a tangled, choking mass of vegetation will result.

This series of charts will help you select both ornamental and native shrubs and flowers for your mixed border. The charts included in Chapters 2, 4, 5 and 6 detail other plants which can be used. Most of the plants listed in this book are fairly easy to establish and can be grown from seed if you follow the instructions and guidelines in Chapter 8.

*Peacock butterfly on buddleia*

CHART 5 **Native wildflowers for the mixed border**

| | Flowering period | Soil preference | Aspect S (sun) Sh (shade) Ps (partial shade) | Height (cms) | Annual (A) Biennial (B) Perennial (P) |
|---|---|---|---|---|---|
| WHITE FLOWERS | | | | | |
| **Oxeye Daisy** *Leucanthemum vulgare* | May-Sept | Most | S/Ps | 20-80 | P |
| **Dames Violet** *Hesperis matronalis* | May-July | Most | S/Ps | 40-90 | P |
| **Lily of the Valley** *Convallaria majalis* | May-June | Fertile well drained | Sh/Ps | 10-20 | P rhizome |
| **White Campion** *Silene alba* | May-Aug | Most fertile | S | 30-100 | P |
| **White Dead Nettle** *Lamium album* | May-Dec | Most | S/Ps | 20-60 | P |
| **Sneezewort** *Achillea ptarmica* | All summer | Moist acid | S | 60 | P |
| **Wild Carrot** *Daucus carota* | Aug-Sept | Most light soils | S | 45-60+ | P |
| **Snowdrop** *Galanthus nivalis* | Jan-Feb | Rich damp | S/Sh/Ps | 15-25 | P bulb |
| **Solomon's Seal** *Polygonatum multiflorum* | May-June | Light | Sh | 30-80 | P |
| **Wood Anemone** *Anemone nemorosa* | Mar-Apr | Most | Ps/Sh | 15 | P |
| YELLOW FLOWERS | | | | | |
| **Cowslip** *Primula veris* | Apr-May | Likes chalk best, will grow in most | S/Ps | 10-20 | P |
| **Tormentil** *Potentilla erecta* | May-Oct | Moist likes acid | S | 5-50 | P |
| **Tansy** *Tanacetum vulgare* | July-Aug | Most | S | 60-100 | P |
| **Primrose** *Primula vulgaris* | Mar-June | Most | S/Ps/Sh | 8-15 | P |
| **Corn Marigold** *Chrysanthemum segetum* | June-Sept | Most | S | 25-50 | A |
| **Dark Mullein** *Verbascum nigrum* | June-Sept | Most | S | 60-120 | B |
| **Wild Daffodil** *Narcissus pseudonarcissus* | Mar-Apr | Moist fertile | S/Ps/Sh | 20-25 | P bulb |
| **Corn Buttercup** *Ranunculus arvensis* | May-July | Well drained | S | 15-20 | A |
| BLUE FLOWERS | | | | | |
| **Meadow Cranesbill** *Geranium pratense* | June-Aug | Most – chalk preferred | S/Ps | 30-80 | P |
| **Bluebell** *Endymion non-scriptus* | May-June | Well drained acid | S/Ps/Sh | 30 | P bulb |

| | Flowering period | Soil preference | Aspect S (sun) Sh (shade) Ps (partial shade) | Height (cms) | Annual (A) Biennial (B) Perennial (P) |
|---|---|---|---|---|---|
| **Cornflower** *Centaurea cyanus* | June-Aug | All | S | 20-100 | A |
| **Giant Bellflower** *Campanula latifolia* | July-Aug | Damp | Sh/Ps | 60-120 | P |
| **Nettle Leaved Bellflower** *Campanula trachelium* | July-Sept | Most | S/Sh/Ps | 50-100 | P |
| **Harebell** *Campanula rotundifolia* | July-Sept | All | S/Ps | 15-40 | P |
| **Devil's Bit Scabious** *Succisa pratensis* | July-Sept | All Moist preferred | Sh/Ps | 60-110 | P |
| **Bugle** *Ajuga reptans* | Apr-July | Moist preferred | S/Ps/Sh | 10-15 | P |
| **Vipers Bugloss** *Echium vulgare* | June-Sept | Most | S | 80 | B |
| **Sheep's Bit Scabious** *Jasione montana* | May-June | Most | S/Sh | 5-50 | B |
| PINK FLOWERS | | | | | |
| **Thrift** *Armeria maritima* | Mar-Apr | Most | S | 15 | P |
| **Soapwort** *Saponaria officinalis* | June-Sept | Fertile | S | 30-60 | P |
| **Red Campion** *Silene dioica* | Apr-July | Not damp clay | S/Ps/Sh | 30-100 | P |
| **Musk Mallow** *Malva moschata* | July-Sept | All | S/Ps | 30-75 | P |
| **Lungwort** *Pulmonaria officinalis* | Mar-May | Most | Sh/Ps | 30 | P |
| **Hedgerow Cranesbill** *Geranium pyrenaicum* | June-Aug | All | S/Ps | 30-90 | P |
| MAUVE/PURPLE FLOWERS | | | | | |
| **Greater Knapweed** *Centaurea scabiosa* | July-Aug | All | S/Ps | 30-80 | P |
| **Knapweed/Hardheads** *Centaurea nigra* | June-Sept | Fertile | S/Ps | 30-60 | P |
| **Field Scabious** *Knautia arvensis* | July-Sept | Fertile well drained | S | 25-100 | P |
| **Foxglove** *Digitalis purpurea* | June | All | S/Ps | 90-150 | B |
| **Betony** *Betonica officinalis* | June-Aug | Most | S/Sh/Ps | 10-60 | P |
| **Hedge Woundwort** *Stachys sylvatica* | July-Aug | Rich moist | Sh/Ps | 30-100 | P |
| **Corncockle** *Agrostemma githago* | May-Aug | All | S | 30-120 | A |
| **Teasel** *Dipsacus fullonum* | July-Aug | Clay preferred | S/Ps | 200 | B |
| **Wood Cranesbill** *Geranium sylvaticum* | June-July | Most | S/Sh/Ps | 30-80 | P |

## CHART 6 Culinary or medicinal herbs to grow in your border

| | Culinary (C) or Medicinal (M) | Flowering period | Soil | Aspect | Height (cms) | Annual (A) Biennial (B) Perennial (P) Evergreen (E) |
|---|---|---|---|---|---|---|
| **Lovage** *Levisticum officinale* | C | Midsummer | Good loam | S | 180 | P |
| **Angelica** *Angelica archangelica* | C | Early summer | Good loam | Ps | 180 | B |
| **Chicory** *Cichorium intybus* | C | Late summer/ autumn | Light soil | S | 30-100 | P |
| **Wild Marjoram** *Origanum vulgare* | C | Summer | Well drained | S | 40-50 | P |
| **Catnep** *Nepeta cataria* | M | Late | Moist | S/Ps | 140 | P |
| **Sweet Basil** *Ocimum basilicum* | C | Summer | Good | S | 20 | Grow as A |
| **Spearmint** *Mentha spicata* | C | Summer | Rich moist | S/Ps | 45-60 | P |
| **Peppermint** *Mentha piperta* | C | Summer | Rich moist | S/Ps | 45-60 | P |
| **Lemon Balm** *Melissa officinalis* | C | Summer | Most | S | 90 | p |
| **Chives** *Allium schoenoprasum* | C | Spring | Fertile moist | S | 30 | P bulb |
| **Comfrey** *Symhytum officinalis* | M | Early | Rich moist | S/Ps | .90 | P Rampant |
| **Fennel** *Foeniculum vulgare* | C | Summer | Most | S | 200 | P |
| **Lavender** *Lavendula vera* | C/M | Summer | Dry preferably | S | 40-60 | E shrubby perennial |
| **Rosemary** *Rosmarinus officinalis* | C | Early | Light well drained | S | 200 | E shrubby perennial |
| **Sweet Violet** *Viola odorata* | C/M | Spring | Well drained | Ps | 15 | P |
| **Borage** *Borago officinalis* | C/M | Late spring/ summer | Most | S/Ps | 90 | A |
| **Rue** *Ruta graveolens* | M | Summer | Well drained | S | 65 | EP |
| **Thyme** *Thymus vulgaris* | C | Summer | Well drained | S | 15-20 | P |
| **Sage** *Salina officinalis* | C | Summer | Well drained | S | 60 | Shrubby perennial |
| **Feverfew** *Tanacetum parthenium* | M | Spring/ autumn | Most | S/Ps | 60 | P |
| **Alkanet** *Alkenna tinctoria* | M | Spring | All | S/Ps | 30 | P |

N.B. Mints, alkanet and lemon balm are very invasive. Contain them in a pot or bucket

## CHART 7 Shrubs providing nectar and pollen for bees and butterflies

| | Flowering period | Soil | Aspect | Height Spread (cms) | Evergreen/ deciduous | Berries (B) |
|---|---|---|---|---|---|---|
| WHITE FLOWERS | | | | | | |
| **Cotoneaster** *Cotoneaster horizontalis* | May-June | All | S/Sh | 150x300 | D | B |
| **Viburnum** *Viburnum bodnantense* | Winter | All | S | 250x120 | D | B |
| **Viburnum** *Viburnum tinus* | Nov-Feb | All | S/Sh/Ps | 300x200 | E | B |
| **Shrubby cinquefoil** *Potentilla varieties* | Summer | All | S | Mat/200 | D | |
| **Firethorn** *Pyrancantha coccinea* | June | All | S/Sh | 400 | E | B |
| **Bridal Wreath** *Spiraea arguta* | Apr-May | All | S | 200x150 | D | |
| **Snowy mespilus** *Amelanchier* species | Mar-Apr | Avoid dry alkaline | S | 600 | D | B |
| **Daisy Bush** *Olearia haastii* | July-Aug | All | S | 120x120+ | E | |
| YELLOW/ORANGE FLOWERS | | | | | | |
| **Orange Ball Tree** *Buddleia globosa* | June | All dryish | S/Ps | 300x250 | Semi E | |
| **Broom** *Cytisus scoparius* | May-June | Most sandy preferred | S | 150x150 | D | |
| **Broom** *Cytisus praecox* | May | Most sandy preferred | S | 120x150 | D | |
| **Berberis** *Berberis varieties* | May-June | All | S | 30x180 | D&E | B |
| **Gorse** *Ulex europaeus* | Apr-May | Dry acidic | S | 180x150 | E | |
| BLUE FLOWERS | | | | | | |
| **Californian Lilac** *Ceanothus 'Gloire de Versailles'* | July-Oct | All | S | 180x180 | D | |
| **Californian Lilac** *Ceanothus 'Autumnal Blue'* | July-Oct | All | S | 180x180+ | E | |
| **Russian Sage** *Perovskia atriplicifolia* | Aug-Sept | Light soils | S | 90x60 | D | |
| **Lavender** *Lavandula* species | July-Sept | Light soils | S | 80x80 | E | |
| **Blue Spiraea** *Caryopteris x clandonensis* | Aug-Sept | All well drained | S | 100x100 | D | |
| PINK/MAUVE/PURPLE FLOWERS | | | | | | |
| **Buddleia** *Buddleia davidii* | July-Aug | All dryish | S | 300x180 | D | |
| **Lilac** *Syringa vulgaris* | May-June | All chalky | S | 150x300 | D | |

| | Flowering period | Soil | Aspect | Height Spread (cms) | Evergreen/ deciduous | Berries (B) |
|---|---|---|---|---|---|---|
| **Escallonia**<br>*Escallonia* | June/Autumn | All | S | 180x150+ | Semi E | |
| **Weigela**<br>*Weigela florida* | June | Rich moist | S | 120x120 | D | |
| **Fuchsia**<br>*Fuchsia* | Aug onwards | All | S/Ps | 30x350<br>180x150 | D | |
| **Mezereon**<br>*Daphne mezereum* | Feb-Mar | All | S/Ps | 80x80 | D | B |
| **Flowering Currant**<br>*Ribes sanguineum* | Mar-Apr | All | S/Ps | 180x150 | D | B |

CHART 8

## Ground cover shrubs and herbaceous perennials

** will thrive in shade of trees and shrubs*

| | Flowering period | Soil preference | Aspect Sun (S), Shade (Sh) Partial shade (Ps) | Height x spread (cms) | |
|---|---|---|---|---|---|
| **Periwinkle***<br>*Vinca major (blue)* | May-Sept | Most | S/Sh | 25 spreading | ES |
| **Periwinkle***<br>*Vinca minor (blue)* | May-Sept | Most | S/Sh | 5 spreading | ES |
| **Rose of Sharon***<br>*Hypericum calycinum (yellow)* | June-Sept | Most | S/Sh | 45 spreading | Semi ES |
| **Ivy***<br>*Hedera helix (yellow)* | Sept-Nov | Most | S/Sh | creeping rooting | ES |
| **Bugle***<br>*Ajuga reptans (blue)* | Apr-July | Most moist | S/Ps/Sh | 10x35 | Semi E |
| **Spotted Dead Nettle***<br>*Lamium maculatum (white)* | Apr-June | All | S/Sh/Ps | 25 spreading | EP |
| **Creeping Jenny**<br>*Lysimachia nummularia (yellow)* | June-July | Damp | Ps | 5x45 | DP |
| **Hebe**<br>*Hebe pinguifolia* Pagei *(white)* | May | Well drained | S/Ps | 30x80 | ES |
| **Wild Strawberry**<br>*Fragaria vesca (white)* | Apr-Sept | Moist fertile | S/Ps | 5x30 | DS shrubby perennial |
| **Oregon Grape***<br>*Mahonia aquifolium (yellow)* | Mar-Sept | All | S/Sh | 60x120 | ES |
| **Cotoneaster***<br>*Cotoneaster dammeri (white)* | June | All | S/Sh/Ps | Prostrate | ES |
| **Self Heal**<br>*Prunella vulgaris (pale purple)* | June-July | Most | S/Ps | 20x45 | DP |
| **Lungwort***<br>*Pulmonaria officinalis (purple/blue)* | Apr-May | Most | Sh/Ps | 30x30 | DP |
| **Elephant's Ears**<br>*Bergenia cordifolia (pink)* | Mar-Apr | Most | S/Ps | 45x45 | DEP |
| **Lily of the Valley**<br>*Convallaria majalis (white)* | Apr-May | Moist | Ps | 20x10 | DP rhizome |

CHART 9

## Additional berrying shrubs providing food for birds and small mammals

All will grow in most fertile and well drained garden soils

| | Soil | Aspect | Height/ Spread (cms) | Evergreen/ deciduous |
|---|---|---|---|---|
| **Cotoneaster** *Cotoneaster frigida* | All | S/Sh | 300x300 | D |
| **Spindle** *Euonymus europaeus* | All | S | 300x200 | D |
| **Sea Buckthorn** *Hippophae rhamnoides* | All | S | 400x200+ | D |
| **St. John's Wort** *Hypericum calycinum* | All | S/Sh/Ps | 30 | D spreading |
| **Holly** (N.B. need male and female) *Ilex aquifolium* | Not wet | Sh | 300x150+ | E |
| **Prickly Heath** *Pernettya mucronata* | Acid | S/Ps | 90+ | E |
| **Firethorn** *Pyracantha atalantioides* | All | S/Sh | 400x300 | E spreading |
| **Guelder Rose** *Viburnum opulus* | Damp preferred | S | 300x250 | D |
| **Sweet Briar** *Rosa rubiginosa* | All | S/Ps | 130 | D |

Also: **Yew, Juniper, Hawthorn, Apple, Blackthorn** and **Elder**

CHART 10

## Ferns to grow in a mixed border

| | Soil | Aspect | Height/ Spread (cms) | Evergreen/ deciduous |
|---|---|---|---|---|
| **Lady Fern** *Athyrium filix-femina* | Moist | Ps/Sh | 60x60 | D |
| **Male Fern** *Dryopteris filix-mas* | Moist/dry | Any | 120x60 | D |
| **Harts Tongue Fern** *Asplenium scolopendrium* | Limey preferred | Any | 45x60 | E |
| **Hard Shield Fern** *Polystichum aculeatum* | Moist preferred | Any | 60x60 | E |
| **Broad Buckler Fern** *Dryopteris dilitata* | Moist preferred | Any | 60x60 | D |
| **Royal Fern** *Osmunda regalis* | Moist and peaty | Any | 120x100 | D |
| **Dwarfed Lady Fern** *Athyrium filix-femina minor* | Moist | Ps/Sh | 20x20 | D |

## CHART 11 Herbaceous garden plants providing nectar or seed

| | Flowering period | Soil preference | Aspect Sun (S), Shade (Sh) Partial shade (Ps) | Height spread (cms) | Annual (A) Biennial (B) Perennial (P) |
|---|---|---|---|---|---|
| **YELLOW/ORANGE FLOWERS** | | | | | |
| **Leopard's Bane** *Doronicum plantagineum* | Apr-June | Most well drained | S/Ps | 60-90x45 | P |
| **Welsh Poppy** *Mecanopsis cambrica* | June-Sept | Lime free well drained | Ps | 30x20 | P |
| **Golden Rod** *Solidago* | Aug-Sept | Most well drained | S/Ps | 60-180x30-60 | P |
| **Yellow Loosestrife** *Lysimachia punctata* | June-Aug | Most moist preferred | S/Ps | 75x45 | P |
| **Sunflower** *Helianthus* | July-Sept | Most | S | 60-300x60 | A |
| **Yarrow** *Achillea* | June-Sept | Most | S | 60-80x60 | P |
| **Polyanthus** *Primula variabilis* | Mar-May | Rich soil | Ps | 30x30 | P |
| **Evening Primrose** *Oenothera biennis* | June-Aug | Well drained sandy | S | 20x45 | P |
| **Californian Poppy** *Eschscholzia californica* | June-Sept | Well drained | S | 15-45x15 | A |
| **Wallflower** *Cheiranthus cheiri* | Mar-May | Most | S | 30-60 | B |
| **Winter Aconite** *Eranthis hyemalis* | Jan-Mar | Most well drained | S/Ps | 7x100 | Tuber |
| **Cinquefoil** *Potentilla* | All summer | Well drained | S/Ps | 30-60x45 | P |
| **WHITE FLOWERS** | | | | | |
| **Poached Egg Plant** *Limnanthes douglasii* | June-Sept | Most | S/Ps | 15x10 | A |
| **Solomon's Seal** *Polygonatum multiflorum* | May-June | Most well drained | Sh | 60-90x60 | P |
| **Christmas Rose** *Helleborus niger* | Jan-Mar | Most well drained | Ps | 30-45x45 | P |
| **Dame's Violet** *Hesperis matronalis* | May-July | Good cultivated | S/Ps | 40-90 | P |
| **BLUE FLOWERS** | | | | | |
| **Forget-Me-Not** *Myosotis sylvatica* | Apr-May | Most well drained | Ps | 15-30x20 | B |
| **Speedwell** *Veronica spicata* | June-July | Most well drained | S/Ps | 30-45x30 | P |
| **Perennial Cornflower** *Centaurea montana* | June-July | Most well drained | S/Ps | 60x45 | P |

| | Flowering period | Soil preference | Aspect Sun (S), Shade (Sh) Partial shade (Ps) | Height spread (cms) | Annual (A) Biennial (B) Perennial (P) |
|---|---|---|---|---|---|
| **Globe Thistle** *Echinops ritro* | July-Sept | Most well drained | S | 90-120x60 | P |
| **Grape Hyacinth** *Muscari spp* | Apr-May | Most well drained | S | 20 Planting depth 8 | Bulbs |
| **Windflower** *Anemone blanda* | Feb-Apr | Rich | S/Ps | 15x5cms deep | Tuber |
| PINK/MAUVE/PURPLE FLOWERS | | | | | |
| **Autumn Crocus** *Colchicum autumnale* | Aug-Oct | Variety | S/Ps | 8-12 | P corm |
| **Spring Crocus** *Crocus spp* | Feb-Apr | Variety | S/Ps | 8-12 | P corm |
| **Shasta Daisy** *Chrysanthemum maximum* | June-Aug | Not acid well drained | S | 80-90x45 | P |
| **Honesty** *Lunaria annua* | Apr-June | Average soil well drained | Ps/Sh | 60-90x30 | B |
| **Fleabane** *Erigeron* | June-Aug | Average | S/Ps | 30-60x30 | P |
| **Geranium** *Geranium* | May-Aug | Average | S/Ps/Sh | 30-60x45 | P |
| **Valerian** *Centranthus ruber* | June-Oct | Average | S | 45x60 | P |
| **Ice Plant** *Sedum spectabile* | June-Oct | Average | S | 30-60x30 | P |
| **Michaelmas Daisy** *Aster novi-belgii* | Sept-Oct | Average | S | 60-120x45 | P |
| **Cosmos** *Cosmea bipannatus* | July-Oct | Light, medium well drained | S | 30-90x45 | A |
| **Phlox** *Phlox paniculata* | July-Oct | Most | S/Ps | 60-120x45 | P |
| **Snapdragon** *Antirrhinum majus* | July-Oct | Light, medium soils | S | 20-120x20-45 | A |
| **Hollyhock** *Althaea rosea* | July-Sept | Most | S | 180-270x60 | B/P |
| **Candytuft** *Iberis umbellata* | May-Aug | Most | S | 20-45x20 | A |
| **Corncockle** *Agrostemma githago* | June-Aug | Most | S | 30-120 | A |
| **Tobacco Plant** *Nicotiana* | June-Oct | Most | S/Ps | 20-90x20-30 | A |
| **Bergamot** *Monarda didyma* | June-Sept | Moist | S/Ps | 60-90x60 | P |
| **Aubretia** *Aubretia deltoidea* | Mar-Apr | Well drained | S | 10-15 | P |

# CHAPTER 4

# Flowery Meadows

## How to create a flowering lawn

1. Plant spring flowering native bulbs in bold drifts in an existing close-mown lawn and leave them to spread or naturalize. The best way to plant bulbs is to throw them underarm in the general area to be planted and then plant each bulb in the place it lands. In this way you avoid the temptation to plant in straight lines or in an unnatural looking pattern.

Plant them using a special tool or dig a small plug out of the turf — keeping it to replace. Bulbs should generally be planted at a depth equal to three or four times their size. The flowers should be left to set seed and the leaves to die back naturally — they must not be cut off for they produce the food which will be stored in the bulb for next year's flower production and leaf growth. To simplify mowing, plant bulbs in bold sweeps so the grass can be left unmown until June when the foliage starts to die back. Normal mowing is then resumed. Odd patches of bulbs here and there won't look good and will also cause headaches when it comes to mowing around them!

2. If you have a weedy lawn, i.e. if you haven't applied weedkiller over the past few years, create a flowery patch simply by ceasing to mow during spring. Plants which can survive for years without the need to flower, such as cat's ear, black medick, speedwell, daisy, clover, dandelion and plantain will send up beautiful flowers. Let these grow for a few weeks and then resume normal weekly mowing. Repeat this each year.

## How to create a wildflower meadow

To create a flowery meadow the fertility of the soil really needs to be reduced, for meadow wildflowers will generally compete more successfully with grass if the soil is poor (grasses thrive best in fertile soils, hence the importance in conservation terms of unimproved pasture).

There are two ways of reducing soil fertility. The most effective way is to strip off the turf and the top 50-100mm or so of topsoil (this depends on your soil type and depth — if it is poor, thin and sandy, or limey then conditions will already be good for creating a meadow). Leave the ground fallow for a while to allow any perennial weeds to grow and then either handweed these out, digging out all the roots (an arduous task!) If your meadow area is large and your conscience will allow it, apply a non-persistent weed killer such as 'Tumbleweed' or 'Roundup'. This is probably the one case where this treatment is justified. Alternatively, cover the ground with mulch matting or black plastic to kill off the weeds but note that this is not always successful with docks and couch grass. The meadow will be a non-starter if it is full of dominating plants such as dock or creeping thistle.

The second way is easier but not so effective and takes longer. Close mow the lawn for several seasons using a grass box and raking off all the clippings, thus slowly reducing the soil fertility. Do not apply any fertiliser.

Finally, sowing yellow rattle will reduce the vigour of grasses which this plant parasitises.

## Converting an existing lawn into a meadow

Adopt the latter technique of reducing soil fertility. There are two ways of introducing wild flowers into the grass sward.

### (1) **Overseeding**

Cut the grass as low as possible in early spring or autumn, rake thoroughly to remove all the loose and dead grass and to create bare patches of soil. Sow meadow wildflower seeds in these patches (either spring or summer flowering depending on which type of meadow you want), and lightly rake in, then roll. This work must be carried out in dry weather. Water the seed lightly as you would if you were sowing an ordinary lawn.

*Gatekeeper butterfly*

During the first year cut every six to eight weeks with the mower blades sharp and set high to leave the sward 7-10 cms tall. This will encourage root growth and prevent the grass from dominating the flowers, but will not harm the wildflowers. Remove all clippings and adopt a mowing regime to create a spring or summer meadow (see next page).

*Greater Knapweed*

### (2) **Planting pot grown wildflowers into the turf**

Hand clear areas of grass and plant pot grown wildflowers into the lawn. Grow these from seed yourself or buy potted plants from specialist nurseries. To plant the wildflowers first water the plant well in its pot. Dig a hole slightly wider and deeper than the rootball of the plant and remove it from its container. Place the plant in the hole ensuring that the neck of the plant is level with the surrounding turf. Back fill the hole carefully. Firm it well and water the plant in.

## Creating a wildflower meadow from scratch

1. Once the turf and top soil have been stripped dig the ground well and cultivate it by dragging a rake backwards and forwards to produce a fine seed bed. Roll the soil to firm it. This must be done in dry weather when the ground is not saturated.

2. Select a spring or summer flowering meadow seed mix containing fine grasses and broadcast at 3-4 grams per square metre. There are various seed mixes prepared for specific soil types. If your soil is naturally damp, i.e. not through compaction from heavy machinery, select a wetland meadow mix. Alternatively buy seed of specific plants you want to grow in the meadow and mix them with non-rye grass mix. It is easier to mix the seed with fine sand to get an even spread of seed. Broadcast half the mixture in one direction and half in the other. Sow in March/mid-April or late August/September, preferably the latter if conditions are suitable.

3. If the weather is dry, water the soil evenly using a very fine spray.

4. Once the seeds have germinated and are fairly well established cut the meadow with mower blades set high.

5. Roll the ground to firm the seedlings.

### Grasses to grow in the wildflower meadow

Avoid strong-growing grass species such as Cocksfoot (*Dactylis glomerata*), tall fescue (*Festuca arundinacea*) Yorkshire fog (*Holcus lanatus*) and perennial ryegrass (*Lolium perenne*), they will swamp out wildflowers.

Include several of the following grasses:

*Poa annua* — Annual meadow grass

*Poa pratensis* — Smooth meadow grass

*Festuca rubra* — Red fescue

*Anthoxanthum odoratum* — Sweet vernal grass

*Agrostis tenuis* — Common bent

*Alopecurus pratensis* — Meadow foxtail

*Briza media* — Quaking grass

*Phleum pratense* — Timothy grass

6. During the first year cut every 6-8 weeks down to 5-10 cms to prevent the grasses dominating the flowers and to promote root growth. No flowers will appear until the next year.

7. In the second spring after sowing follow one of the mowing regimes on the next page and the meadow should flower.

### *Mowing regimes*

The creation and maintenance of a spring or summer flowering meadow is dependent on the mowing regimes adopted.

*Field Scabious*

### (1) Spring meadow

Leave the grass unmown from late autumn until June or July, leaving any wildflowers to flower and set seed and disperse their seed. Scythe or mow the meadow leaving the sward 5-10 cms tall. Leave the hay to dry for a few days — turning and aerating it in the sun to make hay if you want to use the crop for animal bedding or fodder. This also helps the seeds to drop and allows creatures to escape. Remove the hay crop and resume normal weekly mowing routine — so the meadow reverts to a usable lawn, but do not cut it too close. Remember — use no fertilizer and remove all the grass cuttings.

*Ox-eye Daisy*

### (2) **Summer meadow**

Mow the meadow weekly throughout the spring until June. Do not mow closely. Leave the meadow unmown until September/October when the taller summer flowering meadow plants have flowered and shed their seeds. Take a late hay crop (as above).

With both spring and summer meadows it is a good idea to trample over the meadow after hay making to help force the seed into the soil. (In the old hay meadows grazing cattle would inadvertently do this job).

### *Mowing methods*

1. Unless it is a very heavy duty type, a cylinder mower will not cope with cutting a hay crop.

2. For a relatively small area you can use a strimmer. But beware — they are a threat to any lurking frog or hedgehog.

3. A hand scythe is the traditional method of hay making — satisfying but exhausting work.

4. A wheeled rotary mower is probably the best option as the blades can be set at different heights and the action is easier than a hover version. A mower suitable for these purposes can be hired for use in June or September and an ordinary mower can then be used for the rest of the year.

## How to create a cornfield or annual wildflower meadow

While not strictly a meadow, a stunningly beautiful patch of wildflowers can be created by replacing part of your lawn with what used to be agricultural weeds. These are mainly brightly coloured annuals, once common in fields of wheat and barley but now eradicated by herbicides. Occasionally, even today, you come across field corners where the chemicals have missed and where poppies have sprung up. Fortunately poppy seed remains viable in the soil for decades, otherwise it would now be a very rare plant.

Special cornfield mixes are available, the most common being aptly named 'Farmers' Nightmare'. Sow some wheat or barley among your cornfield weeds and you really will create a patch of old England!

The soil of a cornfield patch does not need to be low in soil fertility, but each autumn or spring the soil must be disturbed or cultivated to trigger off seed germination. Sow the seeds in autumn for a spectacular show in June or in early spring which will delay flowering for a month or so.

*Comma butterfly on knapweed*

## CHART 12 **Wildflowers to grow in a summer meadow**

| | *Flowering period* | *Soil preference* | *Aspect S (sun) Sh (shade) Ps (partial shade)* | *Height (cms)* | *Annual (A) Biennial (B) Perennial (P)* |
|---|---|---|---|---|---|
| **Greater Knapweed**<br>*Centaurea scabiosa (Purple/crimson)* | July-Aug | Most pref. light | S/Ps | 30-80 | P |
| **Quaking Grass**<br>*Briza media* | Summer | Most | S/Ps | 20-80 | P |
| **Self Heal**<br>*Prunella vulgaris (Purple/blue)* | June-Oct | Most | S/Ps | 10-30 | P |
| **Field Scabious**<br>*Knautia arvensis (Mauve)* | July-Sept | Well drained fertile | S | 25-100 | P |
| **Common Toadflax**<br>*Linaria vulgaris (Yellow)* | July-Oct | Most | S | 30-80 | P invasive |
| **Ox-Eye Daisy**<br>*Leucanthemum vulgare (White/yellow)* | May-Sept | Most | S/Ps | 20-80 | P |
| **Rough Hawkbit**<br>*Leontodon hispidus (Yellow)* | June-Sept | Most, dry alkaline pref. | S | 10-40 | P |
| **Meadow Cranesbill**<br>*Geranium pratense (Purple/blue)* | June-Aug | Most chalk pref. | S/Ps | 30-80 | P |
| **Yellow Rattle**<br>*Rhinanthus minor (Yellow)* | June-Aug | Most, grow with grasses parasitic | S | 10-50 | P |
| **Perforate St. John's Wort**<br>*Hypericum perforatum (Yellow)* | June-Sept | Most | S/Ps | 30-90 | P |
| **Bird's Foot Trefoil**<br>*Lotus corniculatus (Yellow)* | May-Aug | Most | S | 10-40 | P |
| **Meadow Buttercup**<br>*Ranunculus acris (Yellow)* | June-Aug | Most | S/Ps | 20-50 | P |
| **Small Scabious**<br>*Scabiosa columbaria (Mauve)* | July-Sept | Most light | S | 15-70 | P |
| **Devil's Bit Scabious**<br>*Succisa pratensis (Purple)* | July-Sept | Most moist | S/Ps | 60-110 | P |
| **Musk Mallow**<br>*Malva moschata (Pink)* | July-Sept | Well drained fertile | S/Ps | 30-75 | P |
| **Hardheads**<br>*Centaurea nigra (Purple/red)* | June-Sept | Fairly fertile | S/Ps | 30-60 | P |
| **Harebell**<br>*Campanula rotundifolia (Blue)* | July-Sept | Most poor pref. | S/Ps | 15-40 | P |
| **Lady's Bedstraw**<br>*Galium verum (Yellow)* | July-Aug | Well drained | S/Ps | 15-100 | P |
| **Tufted Vetch**<br>*Vicia cracca* | June-Aug | Most | S/Ps | 60-200 | P |
| **Goatsbeard**<br>*Tragopogon pratensis (Yellow)* | June-July | Most well drained | S | 30-70 | B |
| **Yarrow**<br>*Achillea millefolium (White)* | June-Sept | Most well drained | S | 8-40 | P |

## CHART 13 Native bulbs to naturalise in a lawn

| | Flowering period | Soil preference | Aspect S (sun) Sh (shade) Ps (partial shade) | Height (cms) | Annual (A) Biennial (B) Perennial (P) |
|---|---|---|---|---|---|
| **Fritillary** *Fritillaria meleagris (Pink mottled)* | Mar-May | Wet loam | S | 20-40 | Bulb |
| **Snowdrop** *Galanthus nivalis (White)* | Jan-Mar | Rich moist | S/Ps/Sh | 15-25 | Bulb |
| **Wild Daffodil** *Narcissus pseudonarcissus (Yellow)* | Mar-Apr | Most moist | S/Ps/Sh | 20-25 | Bulb |
| **Bluebell** *Endymion non-scriptus (Blue)* | May | Well drained acid | S/Sh/Ps | 30 | Bulb |
| **Spring Squill** *Scilla verna (Violet/blue)* | Apr-May | Well drained | S | 5-15 | Bulb |

## CHART 14 Wildflowers to grow in a spring meadow

| | Flowering period | Soil preference | Aspect S (sun) Sh (shade) Ps (partial shade) | Height (cms) | Annual (A) Biennial (B) Perennial (P) |
|---|---|---|---|---|---|
| **Daisy** *Bellis perennis (White)* | Mar-Oct | Fertile | S | 7-15 | P |
| **Lady's Smock** *Cardamine pratensis (Pale pink)* | Apr-June | Damp | S/Ps | 15-40 | P |
| **Cat's Ear** *Hypochoeris radicata (Yellow)* | May-Sept | Most well drained | S | 20-60 | P |
| **Cowslip** *Primula veris (Yellow)* | Apr-May | Most alkaline pref. | S/Ps | 10-20 | P |
| **Salad Burnet** *Sanguisorba minor (Greenish red)* | May-Aug | Alkaline | S/Ps | 20-45 | P |
| **Lesser Stitchwort** *Stellaria graminea (White)* | May-July | Most moist | S/Ps | 15-60 | P |
| **Kidney Vetch** *Anthyllis vulneraria (Yellow)* | June-Sept | Most well drained | S | 25-30 | P |
| **Red Clover** *Trifolium pratense (Red)* | May-Sept | Most | S | 10-40 | P |
| **White Clover** *Trifolium repens (White)* | June-Sept | Most | S/Ps | 5-20 | P |
| **Black Medick** *Medicago lupulina (Yellow)* | Apr-July | Well drained most | S | 5-50 | P |
| **Mouse-Eared Hawkweed** *Hieracium pilosella (Yellow)* | May-Sept | Most | S/Ps | 5-30 | P |
| **Common Vetch** *Vicia sativa (Purple)* | May-Sept | Fertile | S | 15-120 | P |
| **Dandelion** *Taraxacum officinale (Yellow)* | Mar-Oct | Most | S/Ps | 5-30 | P |

*Also yellow rattle, ox-eye daisy, rough hawkbit, meadow buttercup, yarrow, meadow cranesbill. For details see Summer Meadow chart on page 33.*

*Cornfield annuals like poppy and corn marigold make a wonderful splash of colour but you must rotovate every autumn.*

*Foxgloves and ox-eye daisies — easy to grow in most soils.*

*Perennial meadow with ox-eye daisy, red clover, buttercup and yellow rattle.*

*Butterflies like this peacock need sheltered suntraps as well as nectar-rich flowers.*

*Guelder rose — an attractive native shrub with bright foliage and berries in autumn.*

*Plant cowslips in your lawn and they will seed and spread naturally.*

*Even small garden ponds may be visited by dragonflies like this male broad bodied chaser.*

*Ponds of all sizes are a magnet for wildlife and people alike.*

*Water soldier and frogbit — two rather unusual pond plants, both rare in the wild.*

*A trough with a mix of wild and garden plants makes an attractive feature.*

*This open fronted nest box was used by spotted flycatchers for many years.*

*Teasels attract insects to their flowers and goldfinches to their seeds.*

## CHART 15 Arable weeds to grow in a cornfield patch

| | Flowering period | Soil preference | Aspect S (sun) Sh (shade) Ps (partial shade) | Height (cms) | Annual (A) Biennial (B) Perennial (P) |
|---|---|---|---|---|---|
| **Poppy** *Papaver rhoeas (Red)* | June-Aug | Most fertile | S | 20-60 | A |
| **Scentless Mayweed** *Tripleurospermum inodorum (White)* | July-Sept | Most fertile | S | 15-60 | A |
| **Corn Marigold** *Chrysanthemum segetum (Yellow)* | June-Sept | Most light soil pref. | S | 20-50 | A |
| **Corncockle** *Agrostemma githago (Deep pink)* | June-Aug | Most | S | 30-120 | A |
| **White Campion** *Silene alba (White)* | May-Aug | Most fertile | S | 30-100 | P |
| **Scented Mayweed** *Matricaria recutita (White)* | May-Aug | Most fertile dry | S | 10-50 | A |
| **Corn Buttercup** *Ranunculus arvensis (Yellow)* | May-July | Well drained | S | 15-50 | A |
| **Scarlet Pimpernel** *Anagallis arvensis (Red)* | May-Aug | Fertile | S | Low spreading | A |
| **Chamomile** *Chamaemelum nobile (White)* | June-Aug | Well drained low fertility | S | 10-30 | P |
| **Cornflower** *Centaurea cyanus (Blue)* | June-Aug | Fertile | S | 20-100 | A |

*Poppy*

*White campion*

# CHAPTER 5

# Pond and Marsh

A well planted natural pond and marshy area will attract a great variety of animals, from bathing and drinking birds to minute one-celled floating organisms. It is bound to be the part of the garden where most time is spent. Pond watching can become very addictive!

## The need for garden ponds

In Britain our wetland habitats are disappearing at an alarming rate through land drainage and reclamation, pollution, afforestation and intensification of agriculture. Thousands of acres of wetland ranging from farm and village ponds to vast tracks of fenland and peat bogs have disappeared in the past two decades.

Garden ponds now provide vital breeding sites for newts, frogs, toads and also many insects — particularly the damsel and dragonflies. All these species are suffering greatly from the loss of natural freshwater wetlands. By creating a pond, no matter how small, you will be helping wildlife in a big way.

## Methods of pond construction

In the smallest of gardens you can create a pond simply by filling and planting up a waterproof container such as a stone trough or a half beer barrel (first well soaked to make the timbers swell and become watertight), or even an old sink! Add 8-10cms of soil or sand and gravel to the base. If you fill with tapwater leave for twenty-four hours before planting to allow the chlorine to evaporate.

## Digging a pond

Whatever method of construction you choose and whatever size your pond it should be dug to have a saucer-shaped profile with gently shelving sides creating a large area of shallow water and a deep area of minimum depth 900mm. This allows pond creatures to survive at the bottom even if the pond surface freezes during a severe winter.

The gently shelving sides have three functions: (a) A large area of shallow and marshy water is created to allow important marginal and marshland wildflowers to be planted. (b) Animals can easily crawl in and out of the water. (c) If the pond freezes the expanding ice will slide up the sides and not force the sides apart (particularly relevant to concrete ponds).

If you are planning a sizeable pond it may be worth hiring a self-drive mini-digger to do the hard work for you. Many of these are small enough to fit through a pedestrian gate, so access should cause no problem, and with a bit of practice they are fairly easy and fun to operate. But unless you are very adept with the machine you may have to finish off the detailed profiling with a spade. Even a relatively small pond can take many hours to dig. Strip the top soil off and stack separately for use in the pond. Use the subsoil to create a bank somewhere else in the garden. Do not spread it over the top soil — always keep them separate.

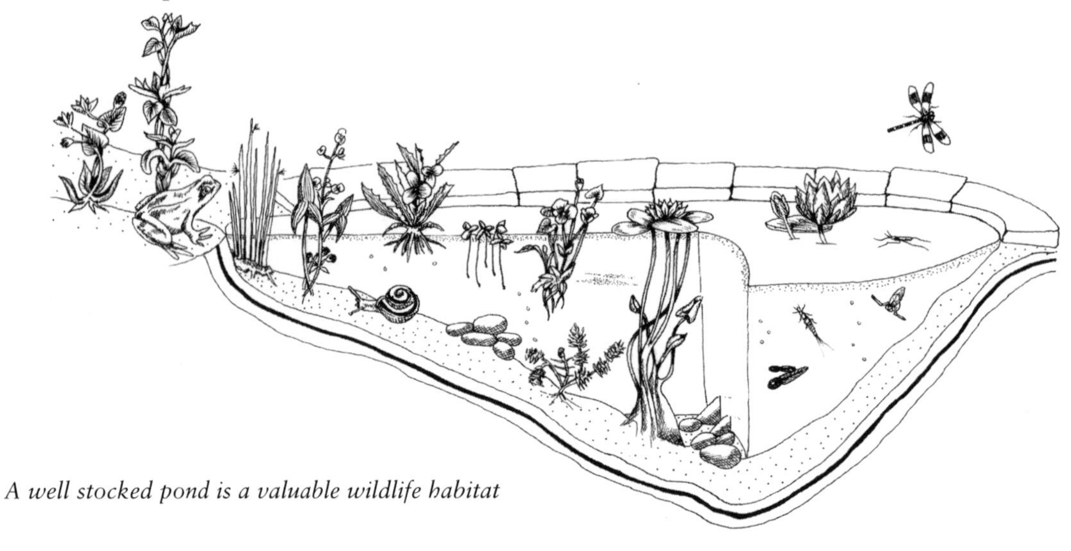

*A well stocked pond is a valuable wildlife habitat*

# Pond Liners

There are various liners available for pond construction.

1. **Concrete and fibreglass** — Ponds are often constructed in concrete but they are difficult to do, may often look unnatural and are susceptible to cracks from frost action. Fibreglass pond liners look unnatural and tend to have steep sides which makes life difficult for animals wanting to crawl in and out of the water. Construction methods for these are therefore omitted.

2. **Puddled clay** — This is the traditional method of lining a pond — puddled clay forms an excellent base for creating a natural pond and for establishing plants. Provided it is not allowed to dry out and therefore crack it is permanent and should not deteriorate. It is a particularly good method if your subsoil is already clay for it is less likely to develop permanent leaks if it dries. Clay for puddling can be bought but the transport costs often make it an expensive exercise. A powdered form of clay called Bentonite is available which is used in large scale construction. It swells on contact with water forming an impervious lining. The manufacturers give details on how to use this form of clay.

Clay for puddling should be laid like paving, abutting the lumps tightly to form an even layer on the entire area of the pond. Water the clay well and 'Puddle' or trample it to form a continuous sticky layer. This takes a lot of effort to get a good impervious layer — it's a tiring job! Then put a layer of soil over this in which to establish plants.

3. **Flexible pond liners** — If you pay attention to the pond edge detail and are careful to hide surplus liner a natural looking pond can be constructed using a flexible liner such as butyl, PVC or polythene sheeting. Polythene and PVC are relatively cheap but will last only a few years as they deteriorate, particularly when exposed to sunlight. Butyl is more costly but will last for several decades provided it is laid carefully. See the instructions in the box. The same method applies to all flexible liners.

### *Buying the liner*

If the proposed pond is large or an irregular shape it may be difficult to estimate how much PVC, polythene or butyl liner to buy. It can be bought in particular sheet sizes so you could cut your coat according to your cloth and make the pond fit the liner! However, it is possible to order a specific size from the manufacturers and if

## Pond Construction

**using a flexible PVC or butyl rubber liner and protective matting**

1. Prepare the site. Dig a hole approximately 200 mms. deeper than the contours shown in Fig. 5a to allow for the sand, matting, liner and soil.

2. Smooth the surface of the hole, removing large stones, back filling and tamping cavities and sharp hollows.

3. Firmly compact the base and sides. All banks should slope gently and be no steeper than 3 to 1 (or the soil will slip).

4. Dig a trench one spade wide and one spade deep along the bank around the perimeter of the pond.

5. The size of your liner and protective matting must be: the length of the pond (+ 2x maximum depth) times the width of the pond (+ 2x maximum depth).

6. Spread 50mm of sand, old newspapers, carpets or a protective matting over the surface of the excavation.

7. Now lay the liner. Handle it with care, walking on it only with soft rubber soled shoes. Don't pull it taught. Lay the edge of the liner in the trench so that it can be held securely by back filled soil (this prevents it pulling loose under the weight of the water).

8. Light must not be allowed to reach the liner or it will deteriorate. So, spread a further protective layer of matting over the liner.

9. Follow this with a layer of a mixture of sand and soil about 125mm thick.

10. Fill the pond. Rest the hose pipe nozzle on top of a square of polythene or matting placed on the pond bottom. Let water trickle onto it gently.

11. Where grass adjoins pool margin lay turves up to the water's edge.

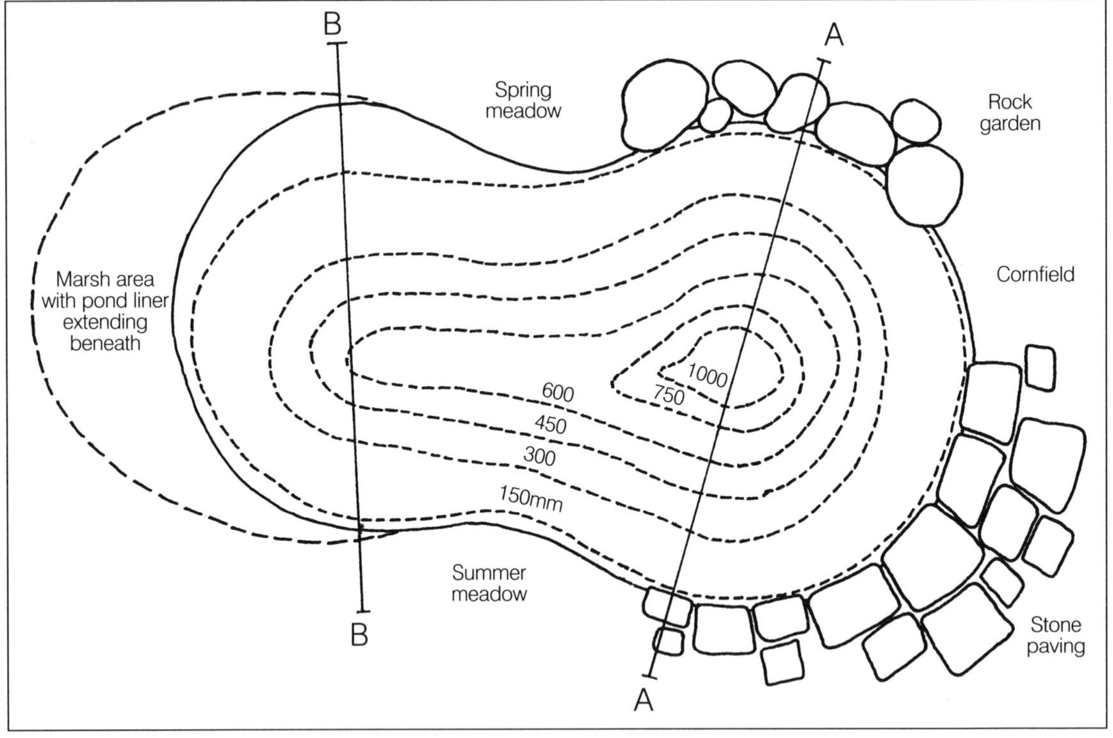


*Fig. 5a Plan of pond showing contours and lines of cross-section*

necessary they will weld sheets together to form the appropriate shape and size. Draw a contoured and dimensioned plan of the proposed pond (as in Fig. 5a) and the supplier will then work out the area of liner required. If you estimate it yourself remember to allow surplus at the edge as the water filling the pond will really drag the liner down, and there must be sufficient to form a waterproof edge.

# Edge Treatment

The detailing of the pond edge will determine whether it looks natural and works efficiently. Try and include various edge treatments to increase both the variety of habitats and the pond's usefulness to animals for drinking, bathing, feeding and shelter.

(1) **Marsh** — When using a flexible liner extend it just under the soil on one side of the pond to create a shallow marshy area. Site this at the lowest point where the pond will overspill in very wet weather. Top it up with a hosepipe in hot, dry conditions. A marshy area (see diagram) can be constructed even if there is no pond. To increase the variety of plants in the wetland it is a good idea to site the pond in full sun and the marshy area in dappled shade progressing to full shade.

(2) **Beach** — Lay a shingle or sand/gravel beach along a gently sloping section of the pond edge — partly below and partly above the water line. This will enable birds to drink and bathe and will provide easy access for visiting amphibians or small mammals.

(3) **Rocks** — Rocks or even a rock garden sited along the pond edge will help camouflage the pond liner and will provide cavelets particularly liked by frogs. Try and site a flat topped rock slightly above the water level and in full sun for sunbathing animals.

(4) **Paving** — A hard paved area will provide a firm footing for pond-watching and for carrying out pond maintenance. Lay bricks, stone, or concrete slabs and leave gaps between the pavers, filling them with soil and sand to encourage wildflowers to establish themselves.

(5) Where your pond adjoins lawn or meadow, try and make the two types of planting merge into one another, e.g. do not have a close mown lawn adjacent to lush pond planting. Leave an unmown meadow strip as a transition zone.

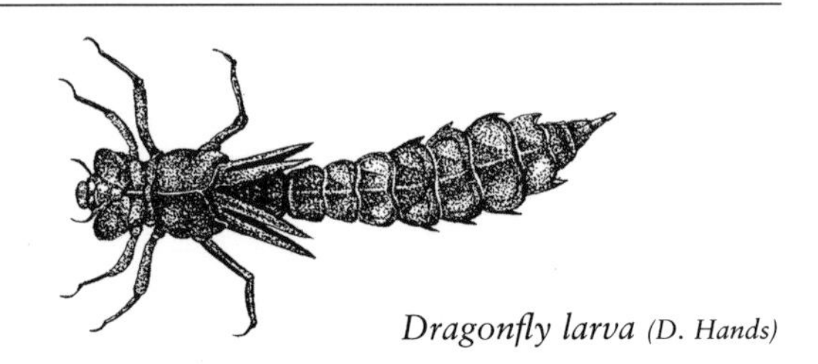

*Dragonfly larva* (D. Hands)

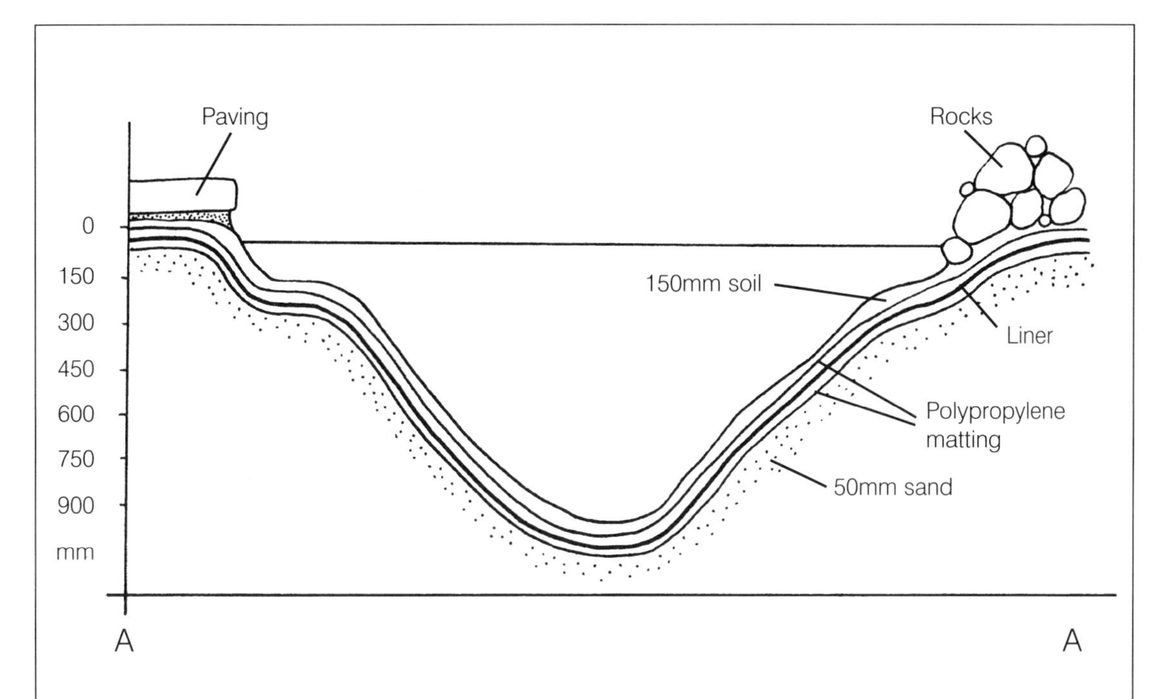


*Fig. 5b Pond section to show profile at AA (see Fig. 5a)*

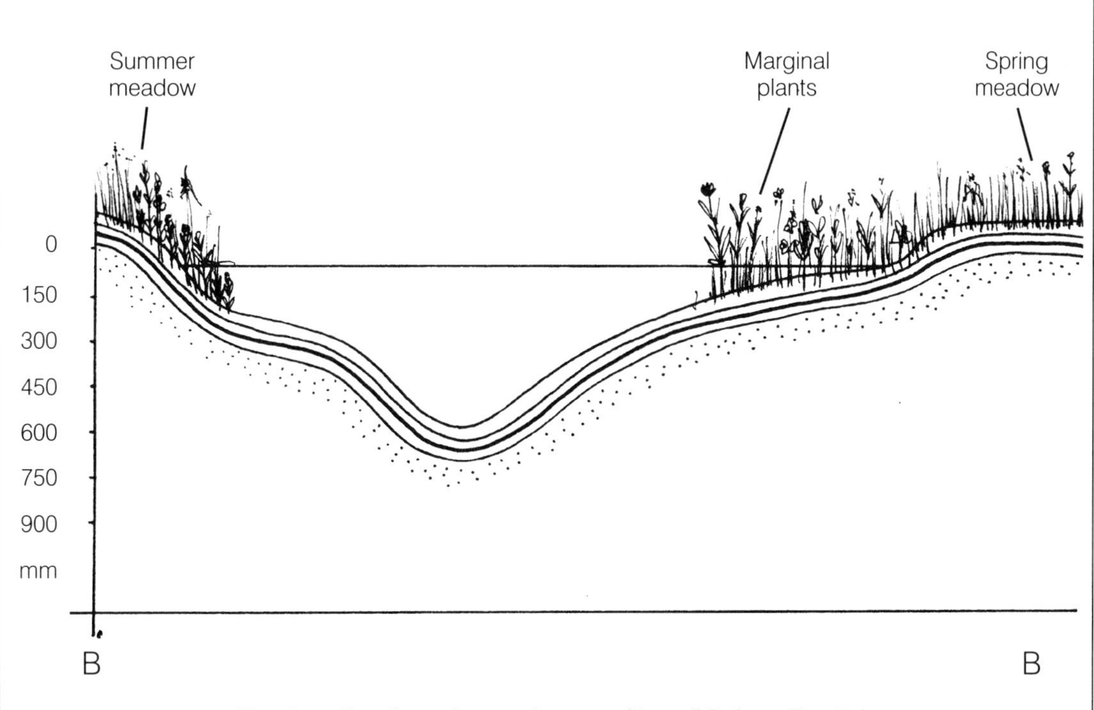


*Fig. 5c Pond section to show profile at BB (see Fig. 5a)*

# Stocking a pond

**Animals** — It is a good idea to collect a few bucketfuls of sludge and water from a well established pond and in this way you will introduce hundreds of creatures into your own pond. However, a word of warning — be careful not to inadvertently bring invasive plants — see the list in the box on this page. It is also no longer acceptable to move frogspawn about, you may be spreading diseases. Let frogs and other amphibians colonise your pond themselves.

Don't stock your pond with fish or they will eat your larvae, frog spawn and tadpoles.

**Plants** — The real success of your pond lies in the planting. Introduce a selection of plants which grow at various depths. The charts which follow give a good selection.

If the pond is small avoid rampant species and grow tall plants on the north side of the pond to avoid them casting shade over the rest of the water. In a small or medium pond it will be worth growing plants in plastic baskets filled with soil to prevent them spreading too much. It is easy then to take up the baskets and split the plants when they grow too large. Even in a large pond it may be worth confining rapidly spreading varieties in this way.

**Growing and obtaining water plants** — Many wetland flowers can be grown from seed but some, particularly those which set seed under water, can be difficult. When buying in pond plants from nurseries make sure they are true native wildflowers and not ornamental varieties. Your best bet is probably to find friends with ponds and get clumps from them when they clean them out. Please do not raid wild ponds, especially those in nature reserves!

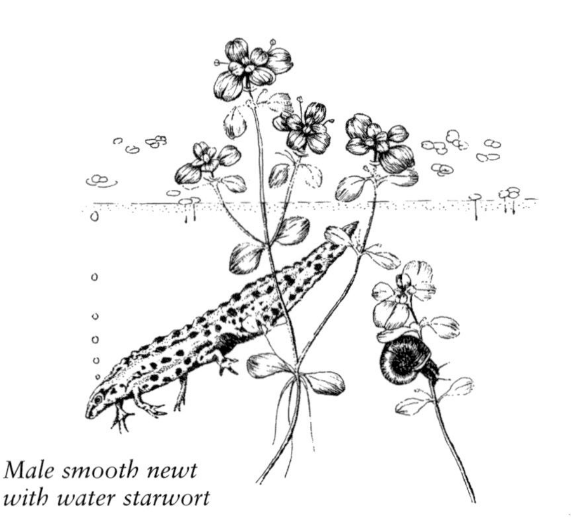

*Male smooth newt with water starwort*

## Exotic Aquatics

Some exotic aquatic plants pose a very serious threat to our ponds and lakes and the native plants and animals which grow there. Introduced from abroad, many are still available in garden centres. **These plants must be avoided at all costs.** They will quickly take over your garden pond and are very difficult and sometimes impossible to eradicate once established. The top ten most harmful alien invaders of ponds, listed by the organisation Plantlife, are:

**Water ferns** *Azolla filiculoides & A. caroliniana*

**Australian swamp stonecrop or New Zealand pigmyweed** *Crassula helmsii*

**Water hyacinth** *Eichhornia crassipes*

**Floating pennywort** *Hydrocotyle ranunculoides*

**Himalayan** or **Indian balsam** *Impatiens glandulifera*

**Parrot's feather** *Myriophyllum aquaticum*

**Water lettuce** *Pistia stratiotes*

**Giant salvinia** *Salvinia molesta*

**Water chestnut** *Trapa natans*

Any attempts you can make to discourage garden centres from stocking these plants will be welcome. Their sale should be banned by law!

As well as these highly invasive and disruptive species, some other pond plants are also well worth avoiding, especially if your pond is small. These include Canadian pondweed (*Elodea* species), water mint (*Mentha aquatica*), greater spearwort (*Ranunculus lingua*), bur reeds (*Sparganium* species), and the reedmaces (especially *Typha latifolia*). In chart 16, the more invasive species have an asterisk by their names. While these can be regularly pulled out when they start invading, it will be a continual battle to contain them.

Other pond plants can also be invasive if the conditions are just right for them and this is something you have to accept with most ponds. Maintenance is at least an annual task with any pond, once plants are established.

CHART 16

# Pond Plants

There are five main categories of water plant —

**These plants can be invasive and may need to be managed*

## (1) Submerged oxygenating plants, tiny flowers but vital constituents of any pond:

| **Water Starwort** | **Hornwort** | **Water Milfoil** | **Curly Pondweed** |
|---|---|---|---|
| *Callitriche spp* | *Ceratophyllum demersum* | *Myriophyllum spicatum* | *Potamogeton crispus* |

## (2) Free floating plants:

| (2) Free floating plants: | Flowering period | Flower colour | S-Sun<br>Ps - Partial shade<br>Sh - Shade |
|---|---|---|---|
| **Frogbit**<br>*Hydrocharis morsus-ranae* | July-Aug | White | S |
| **Water Soldier**<br>*Stratiotes aloides* | July-Aug | White | S |

## (3) Aquatic plants rooted in soil with their leaves floating at the water surface:

| Plant | Flowering period | Flower colour | S-Sun<br>Ps - Partial shade<br>Sh - Shade |
|---|---|---|---|
| **White Water Lily***<br>*Nymphaea alba* | July-Aug | White | S |
| **Yellow Water Lily***<br>*Nuphar lutea* | June-Aug | Yellow | S |
| **Fringed Water Lily**<br>*Nymphaea peltata* | June-Sept | Yellow | S |
| **Broad Leaved Pond Weed**<br>*Potamogeton natans* | May-Aug | Green | S |
| **Amphibious Bistort**<br>*Polygonum amphibium* | July-Sept | Pink | S |
| **Water Crowfoot**<br>*Ranunculus aquatilis* | March-May | White | S |

## (4) Emergent plants for water 15-60cms deep:

| (4) Emergent plants for water 15-60cms deep: | Flowering period | Flower colour | S-Sun<br>Ps - Partial shade<br>Sh - Shade | Height (cms) |
|---|---|---|---|---|
| **Flowering Rush**<br>*Butomus umbellatus* | July-Sept | Pink | S | 150 |
| **Bog Bean***<br>*Menyanthes trifoliata* | May-July | White | S | 10-30 |
| **Greater Spearwort***<br>*Ranunculus lingua* | July-Sept | Yellow | S | 60-90 |
| **Bur Reed***<br>*Sparganium erectum* | June-Aug | Green | S | 150 |
| **Lesser Reedmace***<br>*Typha angustifolia* | June-July | Brown | S | 180-210 |

## (5) Marginal plants growing in less than 15cms of water:

| Plant | Flowering period | Flower colour | S-Sun<br>Ps - Partial shade<br>Sh - Shade | Height (cms) |
|---|---|---|---|---|
| **Water Plantain**<br>*Alisma plantago-aquatica* | July-Aug | White | S/Ps | 30-90 |
| **Yellow Iris***<br>*Iris pseudacorus* | May-July | Yellow | S/Ps | 45-150 |

| | Flowering period | Flower colour | S-Sun Ps - Partial shade Sh - Shade | Height (cms) |
|---|---|---|---|---|
| **Water Mint*** *Mentha aquatica* | July-Oct | Pink | S/Ps | 15-60 |
| **Water Forget-Me-Not** *Myosotis scorpioides* | May-Sept | Blue | Ps | 15-30 |
| **Marsh Marigold** *Caltha palustris* | March-May | Yellow | S/Ps/Sh | 30-40 |
| **Brooklime** *Veronica beccabunga* | May-Sept | Blue | S/Ps | 20-30 |
| **Lesser Spearwort*** *Ranunculus flammula* | May-Sept | Yellow | S | 150 |
| **Water Violet** *Hottonia palustris* | May-June | Pale mauve | S | 30 above water |

CHART 16A

## Marsh Plants

These grow in damp soil at the edge of the pond or in a marshy area:

| | Flowering period | Flower colour | S-Sun Ps - Partial shade Sh - Shade | Height (cms) |
|---|---|---|---|---|
| **Marsh Marigold** *Caltha palustris* | March-May | Yellow | S/Ps/Sh | 30-40 |
| **Bugle** *Ajuga reptans* | April-Nov | Deep blue | Ps/Sh | 10-15 |
| **Water Avens** *Geum rivale* | May-Sept | Pink/purple | S/Ps/Sh | 45-60 |
| **Great Hairy Willowherb** *Epilobium hirsutum* | July-Aug | Pink | S/Ps | 120 |
| **Yellow Loosestrife** *Lysimachia vulgaris* | July-Aug | Yellow | S/Ps | 60-150 |
| **Bird's Eye Primrose** *Primula farinosa* | May-July | Pale lilac | S/Ps | 5-15 |
| **Hemp Agrimony** *Eupatorium cannabinum* | July-Sept | Pink | S/Ps/Sh | 30-120 |
| **Meadowsweet** *Filipendula ulmaria* | June-Sept | White | S/Ps | 60-120 |
| **Common Valerian** *Valeriana officinalis* | June-July | Pink | S/Ps/Sh | 30-120 |
| **Ragged Robin** *Lychnis flos-cuculi* | May-Aug | Rose red | S/Ps | 30-50 |
| **Creeping Jenny** *Lysimachia nummularia* | May-Aug | Yellow | S | Sprawling plant |
| **Purple Loosestrife** *Lythrum salicaria* | June-Aug | Purple | S/Ps | 60-120 |
| **Devil's Bit Scabious** *Succisa pratensis* | July-Sept | Lilac/blue pink | Ps | 60-110 |
| **Meadow Buttercup** *Ranunculus acris* | June-Oct | Yellow | S/Ps | 10-30 |
| **Marsh Woundwort** *Stachys palustris* | July-Sept | Pale lilac | S/Ps | 90 |
| **Grass of Parnassus** *Parnassia palustris* | July-Oct | White | S/PS | 10-30 |
| **Lady's Smock** *Cardamine pratensis* | April-June | Pale pink | S/PS | 30-60 |

*Flowering Rush* *Marsh Marigold* *Ragged robin*

# Pond maintenance

## 1. **Vegetation control**

A healthy pond needs regular maintenance to ensure it does not gradually silt up with plant debris and get taken over by rampant marginal plants. Some water plants are extremely invasive and need to be thinned out each autumn. Most can be pulled up quite easily and donated to friends establishing their own ponds. Where wildflowers have been planted in baskets they will still need to be taken up and split to renew their vigour.

## 2. **Pond cleaning**

It is best to carry out pond maintenance in the early autumn which will cause least disturbance to animal pondlife. No matter how open a pond's situation is, fallen leaves will tend to accumulate in the water. These must be removed before they start to decay and cause pond stagnation. Putting a net over a pond in autumn may help to keep leaves out.

While some dead vegetation is valuable in a pond it must not accumulate. Rake out dead vegetation and debris and pile it up next to the pond. Leave it for a couple of days to allow any pond creatures to migrate back into the water. The pile of debris can be stacked in the hedge bottom or under trees and left to rot – creating a habitat in itself and providing the soil with nutrients, or it can be put on the compost heap.

## 3. **Algal bloom**

An algal bloom — masses of green algae clouding the pond water — is caused by the presence of excess nutrients in the water. Use of tap water to top up the pond can be the culprit.

In dry weather evaporation can cause a significant drop in water level and it is essential to top up the pond. Ideally use water from a stream or water butt, which is feasible if the pond is small and such water is on hand, but usually it is necessary to use tap water. Algal blooms are less likely to occur if there are plenty of submerged, oxygenating plants such as water milfoil, hornwort and free floating plants such as frogbit and water soldier. These will help use up the nutrients in the water. The latter group, together with the floating leaves and flowers of the water lilies, bistort and crowfoot will also help shade the pond — removing light essential for algal growth. The submerging of barley straw, netted up into small bales, will help get rid of algae and also inhibit its development in the first place.

With luck the pond will eventually achieve a balance, keeping the water crystal clear and healthy for the aquatic life it supports.

Finally, if your pond is prone to freezing over in the winter, float some plastic footballs on the surface to allow the ice to expand safely. Don't use hammers to break the ice as the shock waves can kill pondlife.

# CHAPTER 6

# The Paved Garden

THE smallest of paved backyards can become an interesting and valuable miniature reserve. Even without the space for a flowering meadow, copse or pond a wide range of habitats can be squeezed into a tiny plot by using a bit of ingenuity. If space is tight take up vertical gardening. Erect trellis work or a pergola and clothe these and your house, shed and garden walls and fences with climbing shrubs, annuals and perennials. Put up hanging baskets filled with wildflowers, build raised planting borders and plant up pots, troughs, old chimney pots, or sinks with nectar plants for bees and butterflies. Alter your paving so it can be used as a planting medium; dig a pond and build a small rockery or, if space is really limited, plant up a pond in a waterproof trough or tub. Finally, put up a nest box, bat box, bird table, song post, bird bath, bumble bee nest, and a rich variety of animals will certainly arrive in your garden. (See Chapters 7 and 9 for construction details).

## Trellis

A trellis covered with evergreen and deciduous climbing plants can provide nectar, berries and sites for breeding insects, nesting and roosting birds and also for hibernating butterflies. Buy strong squaregrid trellis constructed from tanalized timber (preservative treated under pressure). Good manufacturers will give a fifteen year guarantee on their trellis.

Alternatively, it is easy to construct trellis panels yourself using lengths of rough sawn softwood, approximately 30 x 20mm section, nailed together with galvanised nails to form 150 or 200mm squares. The panels can be made to any size. For economy use secondhand timber (unpainted and usually readily available through your local newspaper). Alternatively, buy plastic/nylon trellis. However, do not attach it to your wall or fence with vine eyes as usual. To secure all types of trellis first attach blocks of wood to the wall or fence with masonry nails or screws respectively, and then nail or hook the trellis to these. Aim to create a gap of about 8cms between the wall and trellis which, when covered in vegetation, can be used by nesting or roosting birds, hibernating butterflies, or by bats. It also promotes healthy growth of climbing plants by allowing a good circulation of air which minimises the risk of mildew and other fungal diseases.

Free standing trellis can be erected as fence panels on sawn timber fence posts (75 x 75 or 100 x 100mm section) ideally supported in the ground in metal post holders (see pergola construction details).

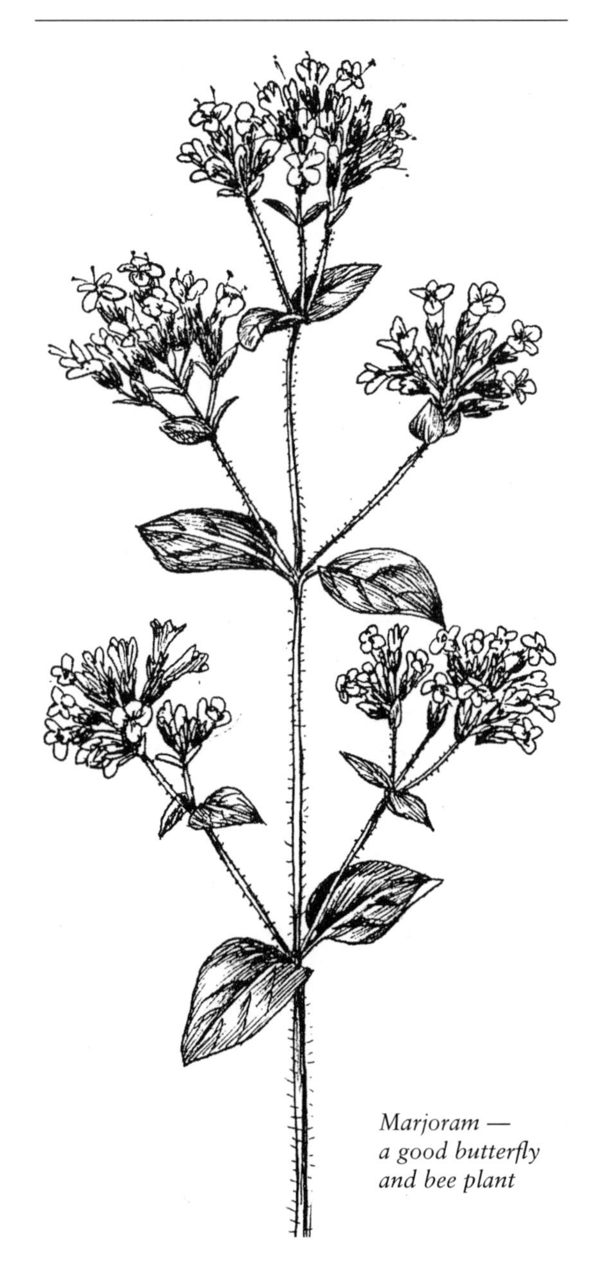

*Marjoram — a good butterfly and bee plant*

# Pergola

A pergola is a useful addition to the small garden being used not only as a support for climbing plants, but for hanging baskets, a hanging bird table, or even a nesting box, as well as providing dappled shade conditions to the ground below.

It may be built against a house or garage wall, or be free standing, and can be circular, square or rectangular, forming a walkway or a semi-enclosed sitting area. Posts can be of various materials — brick, stone, metal, or wood — rustic or sawn. Rustic poles often look contrived and are not longlasting although they do create a habitat in themselves as the wood rots down. A sawn and stained timber pergola probably looks most natural in the context of a wildlife garden and is also the easiest to construct. It will also be the cheapest, especially if secondhand timber is used.

The following pergola design is suitable for a small garden covering an area only 1200 x 2400mm (4' x 8'). The construction principles are the same for larger structures although the cross beams will require heavier timbers.

## Materials needed:

6 posts 2400mm long x 100mm x 100mm (8' x 4" x 4"), preservative treated softwood (ideally tanalized).

3 cross rails 1500mm long x 150mm x 50mm

2 beams 2700mm long x 100mm x 50mm

6 metal post holders

concrete to secure post holders

galvanised nails 100mm and 80mm

trellis panels (optional) 2400mm x 1200mm

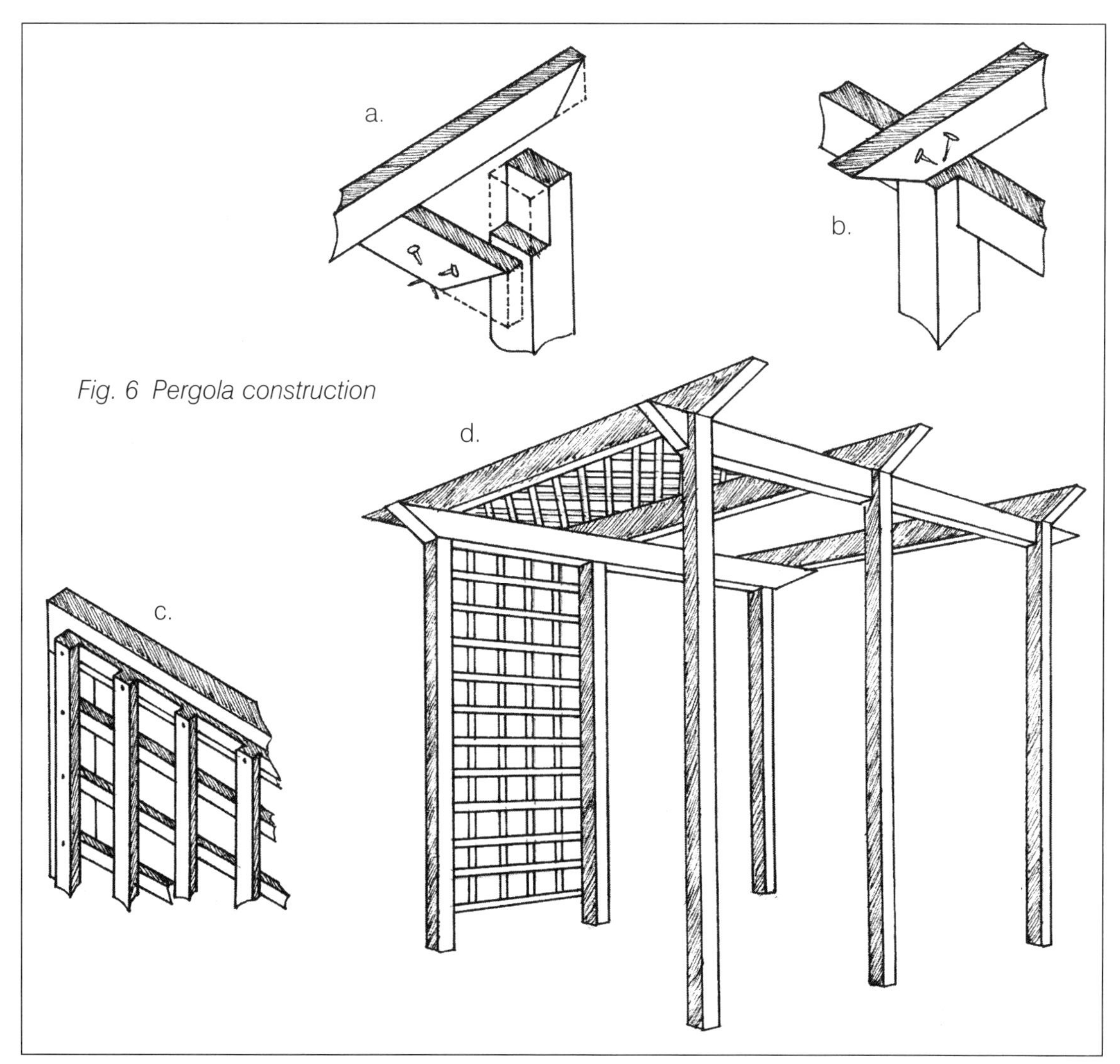

*Fig. 6 Pergola construction*

## Construction method *(see Fig. 6)*

1. Cut a notch 50mm wide and 100mm deep in one end of each post using a tenon saw (see Fig. 6a).

2. Mark out position of uprights. Dig hole, put some gravel in bottom and concrete in the metal fencing post holders. If soil is very heavy it is sufficient to drive in the spike of the metal post holder. Insert a post into each holder, securing with 80mm galvanised nails (notches must be innermost).

3. Shape the end of the cross rails (150mm overhang), and similarly the beams.

4. Fit the two beams into the notches of the posts and secure with nails driven in at an angle through the beams into the posts using two short nails per post (see Fig. 6a).

5. Lift cross rails onto timber frames and secure in position by driving 100mm nails at an angle into the post and cross rail assembly. Drive in two nails from each side of the cross rails (see Fig. 6b). Alternatively secure beams/uprights with metal angle brackets.

6. Fit trellis along the back and possibly one side of the pergola if it is to be used as a sitting area, or omit the trellis if the pergola is to be used as a walkway (see Fig. 6c).

7. Secure wires along the undersides of the cross rails and beams and the inside faces of the upright posts to help you to tie up plants which do not support themselves.

8. Trellis work can be fitted between the horizontal cross rails of the pergola if situated in a hot, sunny part of a garden, or alternatively two additional cross rails can be fitted between the others to increase the area for plant support. Chart 17 gives details of climbing plants suitable for wall, trellis and pergola.

# Planting instructions for climbers

1. Buy bare rooted shrubs and plant them in October to March, or container grown ones to plant all year round if well watered in summer.

2. Water plants well prior to planting.

3. Dig a hole about 30 cms deep and 40 cms wide and mix well rotted manure or compost in the soil at the bottom of the hole.

4. Put a cane about 20 cms away from the wall, fence, trellis or post and slanting towards it.

5. Put in the plant and spread out the roots if bare rooted, or put root ball in hole, avoiding breaking it. Crumble soil and compost over the roots/root ball, ensuring the hole is full and no air gaps are left. Firm it down well, rake the surface over and water the plant in.

6. Tie the stem of the plant to the cane to direct it up its final support.

7. Mulch the plants at the time of planting and in mid-spring with organic matter. Spread it on the soil surface around the plant. This will help to keep the soil cool and reduce water evaporation, so only mulch when the soil is moist.

8. The soil at the foot of fences and walls can get extremely dry as it is sheltered from rain and is usually warmer. Climbing and wall plants must be regularly watered, giving two or three gallons every few days, and every day in hot dry weather.

9. If your soil is very free draining the nutrients in the soil will get leached out so it is important to feed the climbers, especially if they are fast growing. Feed with an organic fertiliser.

10. Many climbers will continue flowering for a longer period if they are dead-headed regularly. Eventually allow flowers to set seed and form fruits.

11. Tie in new shoots of non self-supporting plants.

12. Prune off dead growth in spring or if it appears during the summer. If left on the plant it can cause fungal infection by reducing the free flow of air around the healthy parts. Cuts made in stems should be clean and sloping away from the leaf joint or bud.

*Honeysuckle's evening scent attracts moths*

CHART 17

# Climbing and Wall Plants

## Wall Shrubs

|  |  |
|---|---|
| **Bramble**<br>*Rubus fruticosus* | Train on wires against a wall. Cut out old fruiting canes in spring after second season. Good for insects providing pollen for bees, nectar for bees and butterflies. Berries for birds and small mammals. |
| **Firethorn**<br>*Pyracantha atalantioides* | Train against wall, any aspect. Good for nesting thrushes and a site for an open robin box. Nectar for bees, berries for birds. Thrives in most good soils. |
| **Quince**<br>*Chaenomeles speciosa* | Train against wall. Grow to 2.5m x 30cms thick. Strong branches good for nests — spines deter cats. Nectar and pollen for bees. Beautiful spring flowers. Any aspect, any good soil. Prune back long shoots in October. |
| **Californian Lilac**<br>*Ceanothus (evergreen)* | Grow on trellis on sheltered south facing wall to height of 3 metres. Nectar and pollen for bees, nesting sites for robin, wren, blackbird, thrush, hedge sparrow and spotted flycatcher. Likes south aspect and most well drained soils. |
| **Cotoneaster**<br>*Cotoneaster horizontalis*<br>*Cotoneaster lacteus*<br>*Cotoneaster salicifolius* | If trained against wall or on trellis to form thick growth may be used by nesting blackbirds and thrushes. Berries for birds and small mammals. Nectar for bees. Will grow against north and east facing walls in any soil. |
| **Dogrose**<br>*Rosa canina* | Grow up pergola or on trellis. Nectar. Hips for birds and mammals. Thrives in sun and semi-shade. Grows in any good cultivated soil to 3 metres. |

## Climbing Shrubs (self-clinging)

|  |  |
|---|---|
| **Virginia creeper**<br>*Parthenocissus quinquefolia*<br>*or P. tricuspidata* | Height 7m x 6m spread. Deciduous. Grows in any soil, any aspect. Useful for nesting birds only if grown on a trellis. |
| **Ivy**<br>*Hedera varieties* | Hardy evergreen climber. Grows in most rich soils, any aspect, wall, trellis and pergola. Sound brick and stone walls undamaged by tendrils. Excellent wildlife plant. Nesting sites (especially robin and wren). Hibernating butterflies (especially brimstone). Late season of flowers provides nectar for bees and hoverflies. The native *Hedera helix* is best. |

## Climbing Shrubs (annuals need tying up or training on a support)

|  |  |
|---|---|
| **Honeysuckle**<br>*Lonicera periclymenum* | Train on trellis or pergola in sun or partial shade. Must be kept bushy for nesting birds. Excellent for insects, especially moths. Bark from old stems used by nesting birds. Berries eaten by birds. Like roots to be shaded. Prefers good loam soil and moisture. Flowers on previous year's wood — prune some of these stems as soon as flowers fade.<br>Several ornamental honeysuckles are also useful nectar and seed plants, e.g. *L.* x *tellmanniana*, *L. periclymenum* varieties; Belgica and Serotina. Evergreen honeysuckle *L. japonica* varieties trained up a trellis makes a good bird roosting site. |
| **Old Man's Beard**<br>*Clematis vitalba* | Ideal for trellis and pergola and growing through other shrubs. Seeds for birds. Nesting sites. Ornamental clematis species such as *C. flammula*, *C. montana* and *C. tangutica*, are useful nectar and/or seed providers. |
| **Hop (wild)**<br>*Humulus lupulus* | Wild hops must not be grown in commercial hop-growing areas. Train on trellis or over pergola (or through a shrub). Deciduous perennial. Prefers rich moist soil, sun or shade. |
| **Nasturtium**<br>*Tropaeolum (climbing)* | Climbing annual. Likes poor soil. Good for bees. Seeds eaten by birds and small mammals. Good insect plant. Plant in sun or partial shade. Flowers June-October. |
| **Runner Bean and Sweet Pea** | Climbing annuals — plant in rich soil. Good for nectar and bees. Prefer sun. |

*The paved garden.*

*Herbs and wildflowers growing in hanging baskets and troughs.*
*Ivy-clad walls, bird box and feeder and wildlife pond.*

## Paving

In any garden it is important that paving harmonises with and enhances the planting scheme. Paving in a wildlife garden not only has the function of providing a firm walking surface or sitting area as in an ordinary garden, but it can also be an important planting medium, and home for invertebrates which need to live in the cool and protected environment created.

When selecting paving materials try and use local indigenous materials such as natural stone or clay brick if the cost is not prohibitive, or select small sized concrete paving slabs for economy, for they weather quite well. Secondhand bricks look good provided they are hard and frost resistant. Avoid artificial coloured concrete paving in ornate shapes, and many types of artificial stone effect slabs. Some reconstituted stone paving is acceptable. Real materials always look best and weather down to blend in with the natural effect a wildlife garden should ideally have. With careful planning you can mix natural materials interspersed with planted areas of wildflowers to create an interesting paved area. Gravel used side by side with stone or brick looks particularly good but see the preface on sustainable gardening (page 1).

## Laying paving

The best method of laying paving to benefit invertebrates is to dry-lay it, i.e. on a bed of hardcore topped with sharp sand or, if your ground is firm, simply on a bed of sand. By leaving larger joints than normal between the paving units and brushing sand/soil into the joints, wildflowers can be seeded (and will seed themselves) in the paving (see Chart 18 on page 51). Some areas of paving can be omitted and similarly planted.

If you have existing paving laid on mortar, with a bit of effort you may be able to take up odd areas and dig out the mortar and backfill with soil. Plant them up in the same way. An area of dry laid brick paving needs to be restrained at the edges to prevent it spreading outwards (see gravel section for details of edge restraint).

## Gravel

**Before reading on, see the preface on pages 2 and 3 about the issues surrounding the use of quarried materials in your garden.**

*Hoary mullein — a good bee plant*

Gravel, if well laid, forms a good paving surface which is functional and visually pleasing. It is especially effective if used as a transition zone between a hard paved area or rockery and a soft area such as a mixed border or herb garden. Particularly in the small garden, gravel is an ideal medium in which to grow wildflowers, herbs and cottage garden plants, and many, once planted, will readily seed themselves in the gravel as dust and dirt builds up in the surface layers to give seedlings a foothold. Wildflowers with strong architectural form such as mullein and foxglove, look particularly good growing through gravel.

There are two types of gravel:

(a) pea gravel or river gravel in attractive shades of gold, honey and brown. This can be bought washed or unwashed where it is combined with clay;

(b) quarried gravel. This is formed from fragments of naturally occurring stone. It is sharper edged (and therefore not recommended if young children are to use the area), but looks especially good if laid in conjunction with stone paving of the same rock type.

### *How to lay gravel*

1. Excavate the ground to approximately 75mm if the ground is stony or sandy, or more if it is heavy clay.

2. Gravel needs to be restrained at the edges to prevent it spreading outwards. Bricks, stone setts or timber, are all suitable. It is best to set the restraint on a small foundation of hardcore and mortar to form a permanent edge.

3. Roll and consolidate into the subsoil 60mm of unwashed river gravel or ballast. The clay in the gravel helps to bind it together when wet to become a hard surface.

4. Lay approximately 20mm of washed pea gravel and roll it well in to consolidate the layers.

### *Planting in gravel*

1. With a crowbar, pierce both layers of gravel to make a hole which can be enlarged with a spade.

2. Backfill the hole with good quality top soil, or the soil saved from the excavations.

3. Plant wildflowers in the soil and water in well. Chart 18 will help you select appropriate species although many plants will grow happily through gravel. Scoop gravel over the soil around the plant. This will look good and also help conserve soil moisture.

## Pond

The character and restricted size of the paved garden prevent the inclusion of a really natural looking pond. However, a small formal pond, if imaginatively designed and planted, can still provide habitats to attract a variety of animals.

Fig. 6e shows a cross section of a formal pool constructed using a flexible liner. Follow the instructions for laying a flexible liner in Chapter 5, although of course the pond profile would be different. Incorporate a shelf sufficiently wide to accommodate water plants grown in special planting baskets. The shallow area of the pond can grade into a small rockery or gravel beach giving animals an easy route in and out of the water, while providing winter shelter for amphibians.

It is essential to pay attention to the edge detailing for the liner must be hidden. With such a pond most of the edge will be paved so ensure the bricks or slabs overhang the water a few centimetres to hide the liner. Where a rockery or gravel beach forms the edge ensure the liner is well secured and buried with rock or gravel.

Wildflowers to plant in the pond are listed in Chart 16, pages 41 and 42.

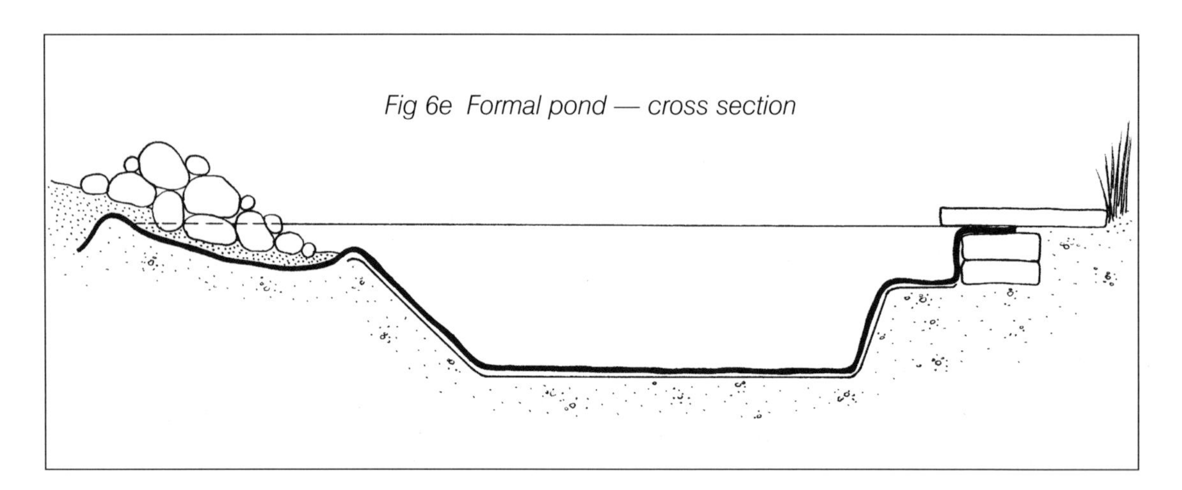
*Fig 6e Formal pond — cross section*

CHART 18

## Wildflowers for gravel, rockery, drystone walls, sink gardens and paving

| | *Flowering period* | *Soil preference* | *Aspect Sun (S), Shade (Sh) Partial shade (Ps)* | *Height (cms)* | *Annual (A) Biennial (B) Perennial (P)* |
|---|---|---|---|---|---|
| **Maiden Pink**<br>*Dianthus deltoides* | June-Sept | Well drained acid | S | 15-45 | P |
| **Biting Stonecrop** (Yellow)<br>*Sedum acre* | June-July | Poor, dry | S | 2-10 | P |
| **Bird's Foot Trefoil** (Yellow)<br>*Lotus corniculatus* | May-Aug | Most | S | 10-40 | P |
| **Herb Robert** (Pink)<br>*Geranium robertianum* | April-Sept | Most | S/Ps/Sh | 10-40 | A |
| **Perennial Flax** (Blue)<br>*Linum perenne* | May-Aug | Well drained | S | 30-60 | P |
| **Basil Thyme** (Violet)<br>*Acinos arvensis* | May-Sept | Well drained | S | 10-20 | A |
| **Sea Campion** (White)<br>*Silene maritima* | May-July | Well drained average | S | 15-20 | P |
| **Rock Cinquefoil** (White)<br>*Potentilla rupestris* | May-June | Well drained | S | 20-50 | P |
| **Alpine Lady's Mantle** (Greeny yellow)<br>*Alchemilla alpina* | June-Aug | Most | S | 20 | P |
| **Bloody Cranesbill** (Crimson)<br>*Geranium sanguineum* | June-Aug | Well drained fertile alkaline | S/Ps | 10-40 | P |
| **Wild Thyme** (Pink)<br>*Thymus praecox* | June-July | Most | S | Creeping | P |
| **Pasque Flower** (Purple)<br>*Pulsatilla vulgaris* | April-June | Well drained alkaline | S/Ps | 10-20 | P |
| **Common Rock Rose** (Yellow)<br>*Helianthemum chamaecistus* | May-Sept | Poor alkaline | S | 5-30 | P |
| **Ivy Leaved Toadflax** (Mauve)<br>*Cymbalaria muralis* | May-Sept | Well drained | S | 10-75 | P |
| **Red Valerian** (Red, pink or white)<br>*Centranthus ruber* | June-Aug | Well drained low fertility | S | 30-90 | P |
| **Thrift** (Pink or white)<br>*Armeria maritima* | April-May | Most | S/Ps | 10-20 | P |
| **Wallflower** (Yellow)<br>*Cheiranthus cheiri* | April | Well drained | S | 20-60 | P |
| **Mountain Pansy** (Yellow/purple)<br>*Viola lutea* | May-Aug | Well drained poor | S | Low and creeping | P |
| **Sheep's Bit Scabious** (Blue)<br>*Jasione montana* | May-Aug | Well drained | S/Ps | 5-50 | B |
| **Heathers** (Various colours)<br>*Erica spp* | All seasons | Acid | S/Ps | Various | Shrub |
| **Mountain Avens** (White)<br>*Dryas octopetala* | May-July | Poor well drained alkaline | S | 2-7 | Woody perennial |
| **Purple Saxifrage** (Purple)<br>*Saxifraga oppositifolia* | March-May | Poor acid | S | Creeping and mat forming | P |
| **Wall Germander** (Pink)<br>*Teucrium chamaedrys* | July-Sept | Well drained fertile | S/Ps | 10-20 | P |

## Constructing a Rockery

Only think of building a rockery if you have access to local and preferably recycled stone. Alternatively, you could create artificial rocks using a coir, sharp sand and cement mix. Here's Geoff Hamilton's recipe, courtesy of *Plantlife*:

1. Dig a hole as a mould for each rock and line it with strong polythene.

   Imperfections will enhance the natural look of the stones you create.

2. Prepare a mix of two parts coir, two parts sharp sand and one part fresh Portland cement. Add colouring powder if you want (yellow works well).
3. Add enough water to make a stiffish consistency.
4. Put some mixture in the mould and work it up the sides so that there's a hollow in the middle. This saves materials and is lighter to lift.
5. After a few days remove the rock from the mould, peeling away the polythene so it can dry out.

If your garden is level you can construct your rockery on a mound or alternatively set it into an artificial bank created by mounding soil against a low drystone retaining wall. This is very useful when space is severely restricted. The wall can become a habitat in itself for bees, wasps, spiders and woodlice. It can also be planted with rockery wildflowers. On heavy soil it is best to construct the rockery as above to aid drainage. However, if rocks appear to be embedded in a gradual slope the effect is more natural. This is easier to achieve if your soil is sandy or gravelly and thus free draining. If it is heavy, dig out extra soil and increase the depth of rubble to aid drainage.

Excavate 30cms of soil (double this if the soil is heavy and you do not want to mound the rubble), and fill with 15cms of rubble topped with 8cms of gravel and 8cms of good top soil mixed with compost and sharp sand in the proportions 3:2:1.5.

Embed large rocks in this, burying them up to two thirds their size, following any strata lines and putting weathered surfaces uppermost to achieve the effect of a natural rock outcrop. Avoid mounding small rocks at random, this looks totally artificial.

## Planting a Rockery

The range of wildflowers that will grow in rockery conditions is vast. See Chart 18 for a selection. Once planted mulch around the wildflowers with gravel to match the rocks. This looks pleasing and helps to conserve soil moisture.

## Growing Wildflowers in Containers

Many wildflowers are adapted to growing in poor or harsh conditions and are therefore ideally suited to being grown in plant containers.

Almost any receptacle from old paint cans to a hollowed out log can be planted up. There are hundreds of styles and sizes of container on the market, manufactured in a variety of materials. Generally, wildflowers look best if grown in containers made from natural materials – wood or clay, rather than plastic or concrete. Suggested containers to use in your paved garden are:

1. Stone troughs are the ultimate container for displaying wildflowers but to buy these is now extremely expensive. However, you can improvise and convert an old glazed earthenware sink to look like stone. First clean the sink thoroughly with detergent, rinse well and dry. Paint the entire surface with a strong adhesive to provide a tacky coat for the surfacing. To prepare this thoroughly mix two shovels of compost with one of sand and one of cement. Add water sufficient to form a stiff mix and spread this quickly over the adhesive (do not do this in hot weather); Cover the sink with a damp cloth so the concrete dries out slowly. Use after three days. Fill as below. Raise the sink off the ground slightly to aid drainage or stand it on gravel.

2. A beer barrel cut into two makes an ideal container - perhaps use one half as a miniature pond and the other half as a planter. Drill holes in the base of the planter to aid drainage.

3. Chimney pots, clay plant pots. These must be cleaned thoroughly. Protect from winter frosts or they may shatter.

4. Window boxes or hanging baskets. Timber window boxes can be bought ready made or constructed easily yourself. By planting wildflowers in window boxes and hanging baskets you can attract bees and butterflies to your house even if you have no garden! You can even grow a miniature wildflower meadow in a window box!

Plants in both hanging baskets and window boxes will tend to dry out rapidly and so extra care should be taken with watering.

Window boxes should be filled as other containers (see below).

The traditional wire basket looks more natural with wildflowers than the plastic non-drip baskets you can buy. They can be hung from walls, trellis, pergola, even the washing line post!

## Preparing hanging baskets for planting

Rest the basket on a large pot or bucket, line the inside with an old woolly jumper and secure it with some damp, peat-free compost. Gradually add more compost up the sides planting trailing flowers through the jumper and wires as you go, securing the roots with compost. Fill the basket with compost (see below). Alternatively, line the basket with green or black plastic — this helps to conserve moisture but does not look so pleasing.

## Preparing containers for planting

For wildflowers to remain healthy their roots need moisture and air, so it is essential that the soil in the container does not become water-logged. All containers should therefore have adequate drainage holes. To aid drainage, cover the holes with a layer of broken earthenware pots or polystyrene pieces. Sprinkle a layer of pea gravel (or limestone chippings if you are planting limestone or chalk-loving plants) over this and then a layer of leaf mould. Fill with peat-free compost. Do not use garden soil.

Plant the wildflowers, either grown yourself or bought (see Chapter 8), and water in thoroughly. Always water well ensuring that the roots are well-soaked.

If possible try and collect rain water from a down pipe directed into a barrel. Tap water may be very acid or alkaline and could affect plants needing specific requirements of acidity or alkalinity.

## Wildflowers to grow

Almost any wildflower can be grown in a container if sufficient care is taken. Mix wildflowers with garden plants which supply nectar and pollen, and group pots together to form beautiful displays and for continuity of flowering. Alternatively plant up a container with a single species for a colourful display, e.g. wild daffodils or cowslips in spring, poppies or harebells in summer. Cornfield seed mixes can be sown in a container and can be very beautiful. Herbs, alpines and creeping plants are all suitable for container growing, as are shade loving woodland and hedgerow plants. Site them to cheer up a dull corner of your paved garden.

Chart 18, page 51, together with those in Chapters 2, 3 and 4, will help you select appropriate wildflowers to grow in your containers.

## Front and roof gardens

Many of the ideas described for the paved garden can be applied to both the front garden or even a roof garden.

It is often the case that the front garden of a house receives sun for most of the day, while the back is in shade. While the front garden is rarely used for sitting or relaxing in it can however be transformed into a beautiful wildlife area. Butterflies, bees and birds will be encouraged into the front garden — and so will you, to watch them!

Grow climbers on a trellis up the front wall of your house. Put nectar plants in hanging baskets or pots. even convert the ubiquitous pocket-handkerchief square of lawn into a spring meadow planted with cowslips or even fritillaries en masse to look stunning. The lawn can be mown as normal from July onwards.

If you have young children and for reasons of safety do not want a pond in the back garden why not dig up your lawn and construct one in the front? Surround it with gravel planted with wildflowers, and so avoid tedious mowing! Then make the front garden out of bounds to children for a few years unless accompanied by an adult.

Before constructing a roof garden, seek specialist structural advice, for example, from your local authority building control department.

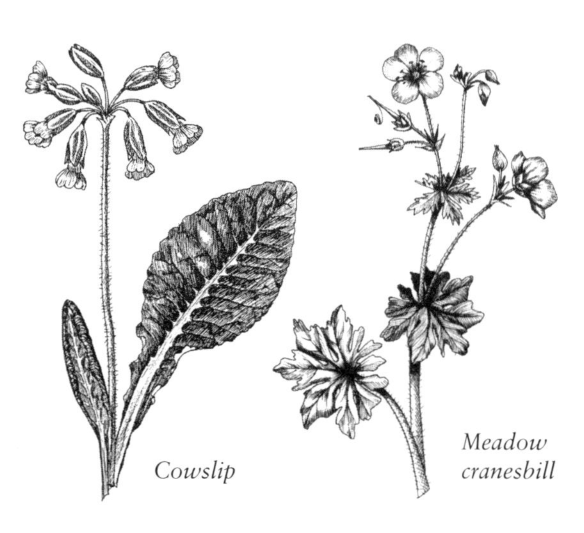

*Cowslip*

*Meadow cranesbill*

# CHAPTER 7

# Artificial Nests

A certain bird or animal may be uncommon in your garden simply because its preferred nesting, roosting or hibernation site is missing. This deficiency can be remedied by erecting artificial boxes. The following designs will help you encourage the more common garden visitors.

## Bird boxes

Birds can be encouraged to take up residence even in the smallest garden by putting up bird boxes to compensate for the lack of natural nesting sites such as holes in old trees.

Garden birds which use nest boxes can be divided into two main categories:

(a) Hole nesters such as tree sparrow, great and blue tit.

(b) Open box nesters such as robin, spotted flycatcher and pied wagtail.

This has led to two basic nest box styles: boxes with small entrance holes (Fig. 7a) and those with an open front (Fig. 7b).

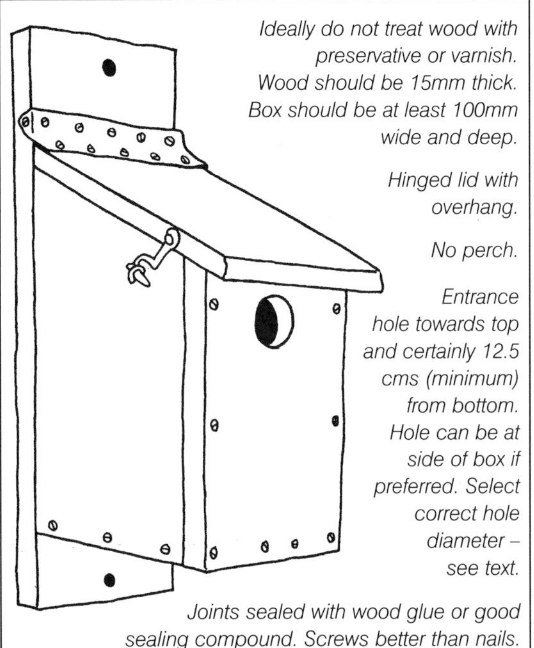


*Fig. 7a Closed box for tits and nuthatches*

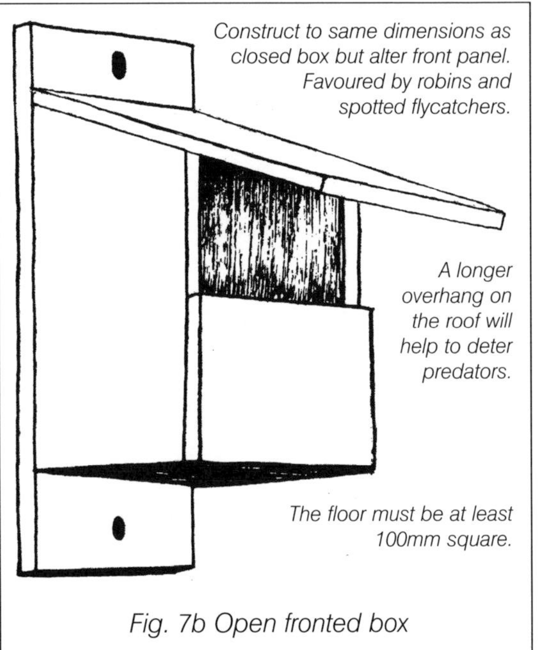


*Fig. 7b Open fronted box*

*Spotted flycatchers use open-fronted nest boxes*

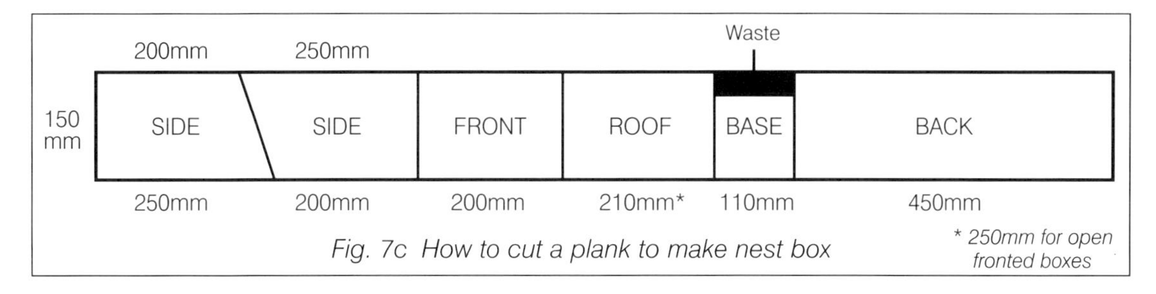

*Fig. 7c How to cut a plank to make nest box*

All are quite easy to make using offcuts of timber ideally three quarter inch (20mm) wood to give a long lasting and well insulated box. Bought bird boxes come in various styles but a simple box constructed from sawn timber is both easy to construct and looks pleasing in the garden. Avoid combined bird table and nesting boxes, and don't put a perch on nest boxes.

Fig. 7c shows how an enclosed box can be made from a single 6" (150mm) wide plank of wood. The diameter of the hole is critical. 1 1/8" (28mm) suits blue tits and 1 1/4" (32mm) will allow great tits entry. Larger holes are suitable for tree and house sparrows.

## Siting bird boxes

Put up bird boxes in autumn or at the latest February so they can weather and so that birds can explore them prior to building a nest in spring. Site at least 10 metres from any feeding station or other similar nest box.

### *Tit box*

Site the box so that the hole is directed away from the prevailing rain and cold winds, and is shaded from the hot sun. Preferably site the box facing north, north east, east or south east. The box should not be in dense foliage and the hole must be positioned so that adult birds have a clear flight path to and from the box. Vegetation and branches nearby will give predators a foothold near the box.

### *Open box*

Conversely, open boxes need to be surrounded by plenty of vegetation. They can be fixed to walls (but not too near the roof or windowsill), to strong trellis where they can be hidden by climbing shrubs or in suitable crotch sites in trees. Alternatively these boxes can be fitted inside a shed or garage if the door or window is left open.

Both types must not be less than two metres above the ground.

Fig. 7d shows an artificial house martin nest.

## Cleaning out nest boxes

Old nests in closed boxes can harbour flea pupae which may infect young birds in the following year unless removed. Clean out the box in the autumn. Do not fumigate it with insecticides or flea powders — boiling water will do the trick.

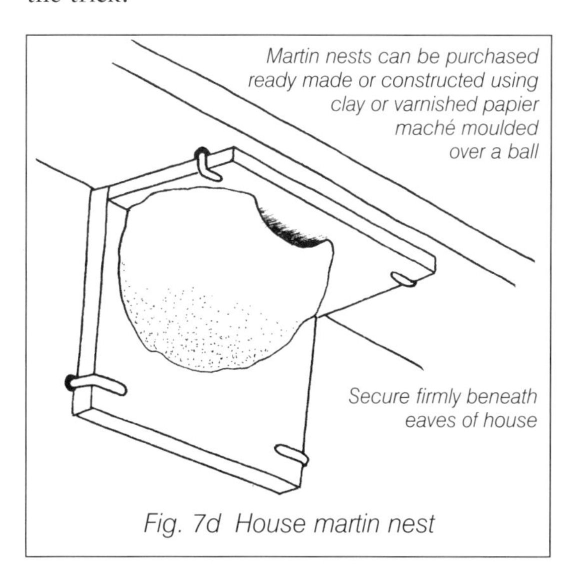

*Fig. 7d House martin nest*

## Bumblebees

Bumblebees are increasingly under threat from intensive use of the land and modern farming practices which have resulted in the loss of rough grassland, banks and hedgerows — all favoured by bees for nesting. Moreover the use of herbicides has reduced the nectar and pollen supply.

In the garden there are several steps you can take to help bumblebees:

1. Grow the right varieties of plants to ensure a continuous supply of food from March to September; especially summer flowering delphiniums, snapdragons, ceanothus, comfrey, clover, honeysuckle, hollyhock, borage and cotoneaster, and for early spring; goat willow, white deadnettle, and flowering currant. (See list of nectar plants in Chapter 3).

2. Provide nesting and hibernation sites in the garden; rotting wood, piles of cut vegetation, mounds of earth and rubble, a drystone wall or rockery.

Leave areas of undisturbed rough ground which bumblebees like. They will nest in warm, dry, south facing hummocks, especially in old mouse or vole nests. This is obviously only possible in a large garden.

3. Even in a small garden you can encourage bumblebees by constructing an artificial nest box. The basic requirements for a bumblebee nest are a dry, well drained and insulated space about the size of a football, containing some soft, dry bedding material.

There are various designs of nest box. Probably the simplest method of construction is to use a 9 inch (22.5 cm) flower pot and a piece of hosepipe (see Fig. 7e). Two thirds fill the pot with material from an old mouse nest or old bedding from a pet hamster or gerbil. Alternatively use furniture stuffing or fresh animal bedding. Do not use cotton wool as bees get their feet tangled up in it. Bury the pot at an angle in banked up soil in a sunny and private part of the garden (bees are very modest!) Alternatively bury the pot in a level stretch of ground and cover it with a slate raised up with two stones to form an entrance. Make sure that the bumblebees' nest is ready by late March or early April when the queen bee starts to look for a suitable site.

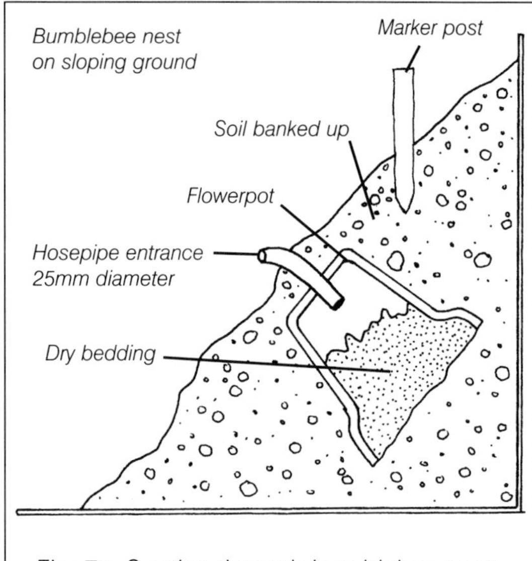


*Fig. 7e Section through bumblebee nest*

## Hedgehogs

Hedgehogs can be encouraged to take up residence by providing suitable hibernation sites even as simple as a pile of leaves and twigs in an undisturbed corner of the garden.

A hibernation box can be constructed fairly simply and if this is adequately insulated and waterproofed it may also be used by the hedgehog for making a nest and rearing her young, or even for sleeping in during the day (see Fig. 7f).

The box should be made of untreated timber with approximate dimensions 30 x 40 x 30 cms high. Construct an entrance tunnel 14 cms square to prevent dogs, cats, or even foxes, entering the box.

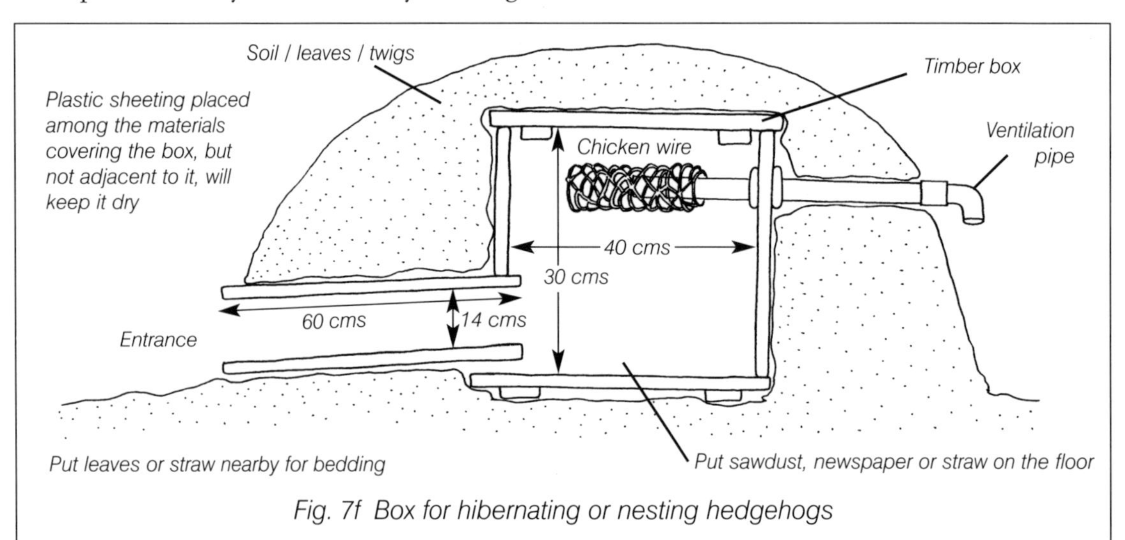


*Fig. 7f Box for hibernating or nesting hedgehogs*

To prevent condensation from wetting the inside of the box it must have a ventilation pipe. An old plastic or metal water pipe can be used for this. To ensure the pipe doesn't get blocked with bedding material securely fix chicken wire around the end.

To prevent water penetrating and soaking the box, cover it with polythene but do not seal it or the condensation problem will be aggravated. The whole box can be covered with a mound of soil about 30 cms deep, or with leaves piled over with dead twigs, etc. This will protect, disguise and insulate the hedgehog box.

## Bats

Bats are much misunderstood mammals, and in recent years have declined rapidly in numbers. Different species of bat hibernate or roost in locations such as caves, trees and in roof spaces. Disturbance, loss of woodland, the treatment of roof timbers with preservatives and the fumigation of lofts have led to the demise of bats. They are now legally protected.

Try to encourage bats into your house by making a small slit in the soffit on your eaves which will give them access to the space between the soffit and bargeboard, or into the roof space itself. Bats do no damage (their droppings are small and dry) and by doing this you really will be making a positive contribution to wildlife conservation.

Alternatively you can build special bat boxes to fix to your wall or roof (see Fig. 7g). The bat box resembles an enclosed bird box but omit the hole and substitute a narrow slit about 15mm wide underneath. The box should have a 100mm x 100mm floorspace. Use rough sawn timber that has not been painted or treated with creosote or preservatives (lethal to bats).

The backboard of the box should be sawn to produce shallow horizontal grooves to enable the bats to cling on better. Boxes should be sited a minimum of three metres from the ground and preferably higher to reduce the risk of interference.

Bats are very particular about the exact temperature and humidity they require. So don't expect a high occupancy rate or indeed any occupancy at all! Do put up at least three boxes on the same tree, facing north, east and west respectively. This may increase your chances of getting bats to use them. Boxes for use by hibernating bats need to be made of much thicker wood —100mm or so thick is best.

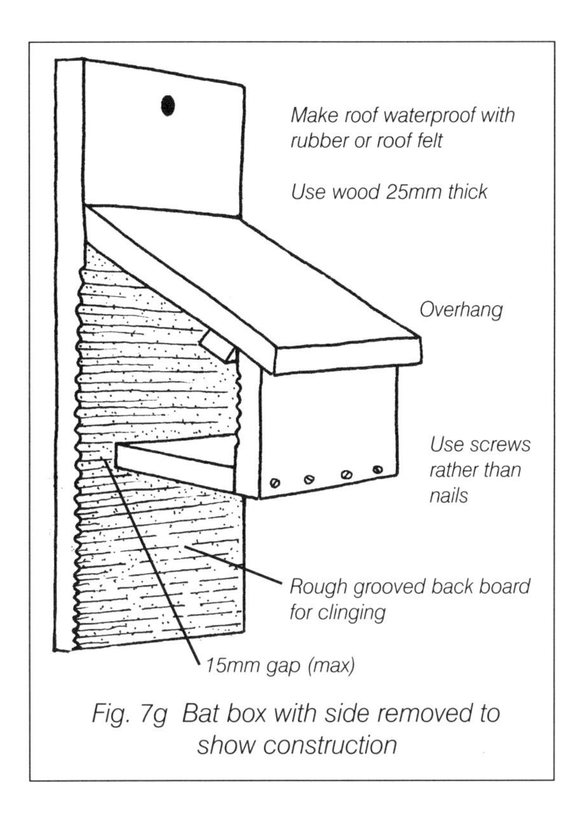


*Fig. 7g Bat box with side removed to show construction*

## Insect chambers and hibernacula

Many designs of structures for breeding and hibernating insects are available from specialist firms or they can be constructed at home.

These range from bundles of hollow sticks tied together and hung on a wall to rather elaborate and expensive lacewing boxes, impregnated with special attractants. Also, do remember to leave as many seedheads and dead plant stems (especially hollow ones) throughout the winter. Ladybirds, lacewings and many other insects and their larvae will survive better if you do.

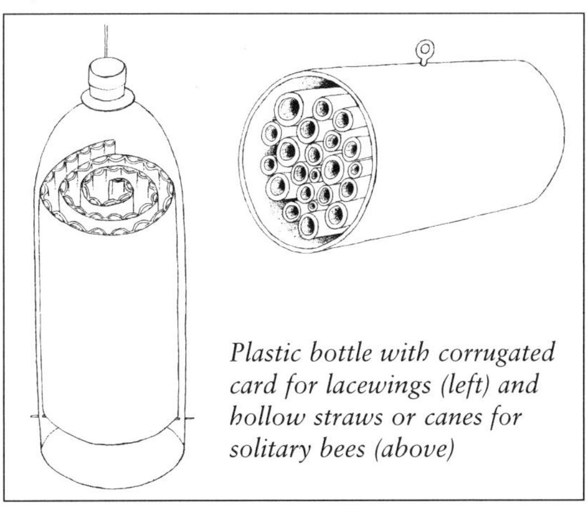

*Plastic bottle with corrugated card for lacewings (left) and hollow straws or canes for solitary bees (above)*

# CHAPTER 8

# Plant Propagation

BUYING pot grown or bare rooted wildflowers, trees and shrubs from nurseries, garden centres, or specialist growers can be a frustrating exercise as many are unavailable or very expensive, particularly if you have an entire garden to plant up. Growing your plants from seed or cuttings gathered yourself or given by friends is not only satisfying but also a much cheaper way of stocking your plot. In this way there is a greater chance of your plants being of native origin. It is illegal to take plants from the wild but seeds can be collected with the landowner's permission.

## A. Cuttings

If you grow shrubs, trees and perennials from seed then it will be several years before you have a reasonable sized plant. It's well worth doing nonetheless, but growing them from hardwood and softwood cuttings speeds up the process. Most parts of a plant can be used as cuttings and grown on to form a replica of the plant. Hard and softwood cuttings are probably the easiest and most useful.

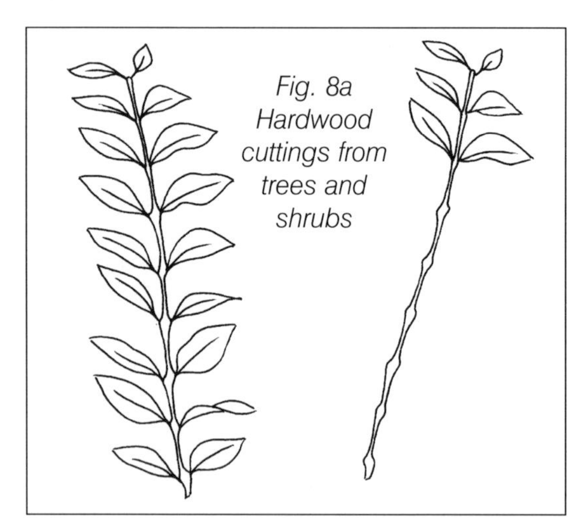

*Fig. 8a Hardwood cuttings from trees and shrubs*

**A hardwood cutting** is a stem cutting from fully mature wood taken at the end of the growing season from current year's growth. Hardwood cuttings are planted in the open ground to make roots before being planted in their permanent positions the following year.

(1) Cut a portion of stem 25-30 cms long, cutting at immediately below a node or joint.

(2) With a sharp knife remove leaves, stalks and buds from two thirds of the stem, i.e. the part which will be inserted into the soil. (Fig 8a).

(3) Dip cut end into root-promoting hormone powder.

(4) Dig a trench about 20 cms deep, sprinkle coarse sand in the bottom to encourage rooting.

(5) Place the cuttings against one side of the trench. Replace the soil and firm it in.

(6) In severe weather the cuttings can be covered with a cloche. If frost loosens them firm them back. The cuttings will remain dormant throughout the winter and will produce roots in the following spring.

*Fig. 8b Softwood cuttings from trees, shrubs and woody perennials*

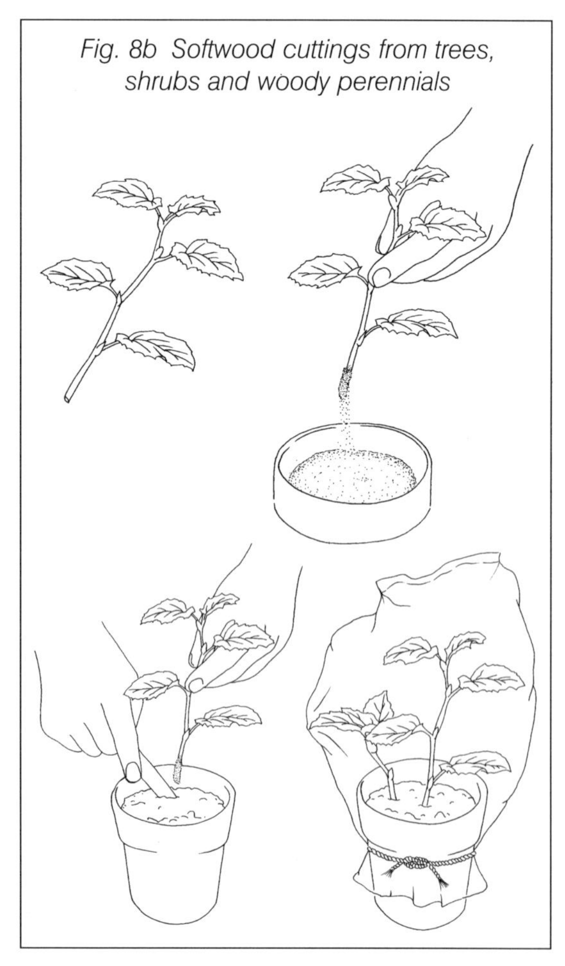

**A softwood cutting** is a stem cutting taken early on in the growing season while the shoots are soft and sappy. The moisture in these cuttings evaporates rapidly so they must be rooted in a damp atmosphere under cover.

(1) Take a cutting 5-6 cms long and prepare as hardwood cutting (1 and 2 above).

(2) Insert the cuttings in pots or a tray filled with a light, sandy compost.

(3) Water with a fine rose on the can.

(4) Place in a plastic bag (or propagating frame if you have one) on a warm windowsill or greenhouse. (Fig. 8b). Shade from direct sunshine.

(5) As soon as the cuttings have rooted (give them a gentle pull to see) pot them on into clean pots or boxes filled with a light potting compost. Keep the new small plants moist and shade them from strong light.

(6) Gradually harden them off by moving them into colder temperatures and less shade until they can be planted out into their permanent positions.

## B. Plant division

This is a vegetative propagation method whereby plants are separated into smaller plants, each complete with roots and growth buds. It is the easiest method of increase most perennials and is carried out during the winter dormant period, or at the beginning of the new growing season.

(a) *Suckers.* Some shrubs such as blackthorn and wild roses produce suckers — shoots which arise below ground at the base of the plant and which produce new plants attached to the parent. These can be dug up, severed from the parent plant and replanted in spring or autumn.

(b) *Runners.* Several shrubby plants send out horizontal overground shoots or stolons, which root where they touch the soil and produce new plants which can be detached from the parent plant and planted out in the spring or autumn.

(c) *Offsets.* These are small complete plants produced by many bulbous plants such as bluebells, wild daffodils and fritillaries. Offsets are attached to the parent bulbs or corms and when detached by hand and planted elsewhere they will form large bulbs or corms which will flower after a couple of years. It is best to detach these when the flower has finished flowering and the leaves are dying back.

(d) *Division by splitting.* Most perennial wildflowers can be increased by splitting the plant into pieces. Dig the plant up in the dormant season (autumn/winter) or at the beginning of the new growing season. Shake off the soil and pull it apart into several portions each retaining a number of roots and at least one shoot or growth bud. Tough clumps which cannot be easily torn apart can be divided with the aid of two forks. Drive the forks, back to back, through the clump and lever it apart. Dividing your herbaceous perennials in this way will not only increase your stock but will promote healthy growth; many perennials are not very long lived.

## C. Layering

Layering is a method of vegetative propagation where a stem attached to the plant is induced to form roots and eventually produce an independent plant. An example of layering is this tip layering of blackberries.

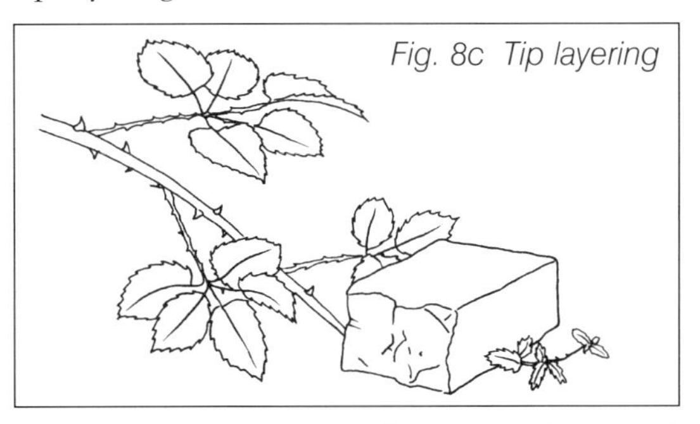
*Fig. 8c Tip layering*

Choose a young non-flowering shoot and check the flow of sap by twisting or bending the stem at the point where it will make contact with the soil. Strip off the leaves from the part of stem or branch that will be in contact with the soil. Press the injured part into the soil — adding some sand to the soil at this point. Anchor the shoot by pegging it with wooden or wire pegs or putting a large stone or brick on it. Firstly, cover the injured part with soil and water it thoroughly. Once the stem has rooted itself you can sever the stem, so detaching it from the parent plant, and after a few days it can be planted in its permanent position.

Layering is a useful method of increasing your stock of bramble, heathers, ivy, clematis, and honeysuckle.

## D. Growing wildflowers from seed

Undoubtedly the best and cheapest way to increase your stocks of annuals and perennials is to collect or buy seed and germinate it yourself.

The wildflowers that can be grown most easily in your garden and that have the best chance of flourishing are those that are locally common as they are already well adapted to local conditions. However, it is not wise to collect seed from the countryside unless the plant concerned is very common and locally abundant. It is very easy to gather seed from some wonderful wildflower and in doing so, inadvertently trample surrounding plants or even damage the parent plant. If there is only a single colony, then by collecting seed you will be preventing the plant from spreading within its natural surroundings. It is, in fact, illegal to collect seed from certain rare plants so as a rule avoid collecting from the wild. (As a wildlife gardener you should be helping to grow additional wildflowers — not depleting the already diminishing native stock).

It is also illegal to dig up wild plants from the countryside. Most, and probably all, the wildflowers you will want to grow in your garden, and certainly all those mentioned in this book are readily available as seedlings or seeds by post from various seed merchants and good garden centres (see list on pages 68 and 69).

Once you have a few wildflowers established you can then collect your own seed. Try and get to know other wildflower gardeners in your area (your local wildlife trust may be able to suggest a few names) and then you will be able to swop and barter for your seeds and seedlings.

(a) **Harvesting wildflower seed.** Judging the correct time to collect seed can be difficult. All plants have specialised methods of seed dispersal. By understanding these mechanisms and knowing when the plant's flowering period is likely to be over you will be well on the way to working out how and when to harvest your seed.

Many seeds are ready for harvesting when the fruit or seed head is brown and dry (as with poppies and cowslips) or dry and fluffy (like thistles and dandelions), but others will need more careful inspection. Some seed heads need to be gathered even before the seeds are fully ripe in order to catch the seeds before they are physically expelled from the fruit, e.g. knapweed and members of the cranesbill family.

(b) Harvesting tree and shrub seed. Whereas trees and shrubs can be propagated more quickly from cuttings this always results in a plant identical to the parent. By growing them from seed each plant will vary slightly from the next.

Unlike many wildflowers the seed of trees and shrubs usually stays in the fruit attached to the plant for some time. This makes collection much easier. Generally tree seed is in the form of hard fruit or nuts (oak, hazel, beech), fleshy fruits (hawthorn, crab apple, blackthorn, honeysuckle, guelder rose, bramble, wild rose, elderberry, wild privet, holly, rowan) catkins (silver birch, goat willow), or keys (ash, field maple).

Most tree seeds are best sown directly into the ground in autumn (see method below). Where berried fruits are concerned you must extract the seed from the flesh either by pulping down the fruit in a sieve or in a food blender if the seed is very small and won't be damaged.

(c) **Sowing seed.** If you have collected your own seed it is best to sow it in seed trays or straight into the ground while it is fresh as it would be sown in the wild. However, you may have reason to keep it until spring, in which case it is vital that you keep it perfectly dry and dark and at an even temperature.

Bought or stored seed may be in a dormant state. Seed undergoes various changes to allow it to remain viable, often for many years, until conditions are right for it to germinate. Such seed may need special treatment to encourage it. One of the following two methods may be necessary:

*Scarification* — This technique of rubbing hard coated seed between two sheets of sandpaper helps to break down the seed coat so allowing moisture to penetrate through to the seed — essential for germination of seeds from cranesbills and vetches, etc.

*Stratification* — Many seeds need to undergo a period of cold for a specific time before they will germinate. The list includes holly, ivy, poppy and many roses. If seed is sown in autumn directly into the ground or in seed trays which are covered with glass but left in the open air, then the seed automatically undergoes stratification. However, you can simulate the winter weather by putting the seed with dry sand in plastic bags in the fridge for 1-3 months, although this may be unsuccessful as certain seed needs fluctuating temperatures to germinate.

*Sowing seed in the open ground* — This is best for larger seeds. If you intend to sow your seed in the open ground you must ensure that the soil is in a suitable condition, i.e. not too cold and wet, conditions which will delay germination.

1) Prepare the ground by firming the soil and raking it evenly to create a fine tilth ensuring it is weed free.

2) Sow seeds in shallow drills made by pressing a hoe handle lightly on the surface, or broadcast evenly and thinly. In dry weather lightly water the drills or area to be sown.

3) Cover drills or seed lightly with soil by raking gently.

4) Label and date the seed!

5) Keep weeds and birds at bay.

## Sowing small seeds in pots and trays *(Fig. 8d)*

1. Clean the seed trays or pots thoroughly and put a layer of broken crocks in the base. Fill up with a proprietary seed compost, or a sandy compost mixture (one part leafmould, one part coarse sand, 2 parts sifted loam) nearly to the rim. Firm the compost to an even surface.

2. Water the trays thoroughly by immersing in water to below the container rim or by using a watering can and fine rose. Drain well.

3. Sow the seed very thinly and evenly to the appropriate depth. Generally seeds should be sown to a depth equal to their thickness, though larger seed such as acorns should be sown approximately 60mm deep as they tend to move towards the surface as they germinate. Space larger seeds 1 cm apart.

Sprinkle some fine silver sand or compost over the tray. Dust-like seeds such as harebell (you need a magnifying glass to see them) need no covering of soil at all.

4. Cover with a sheet of plastic or glass or put in a plastic bag. Then place in a sheltered lightly shaded spot outdoors or in a cold frame or unheated greenhouse.

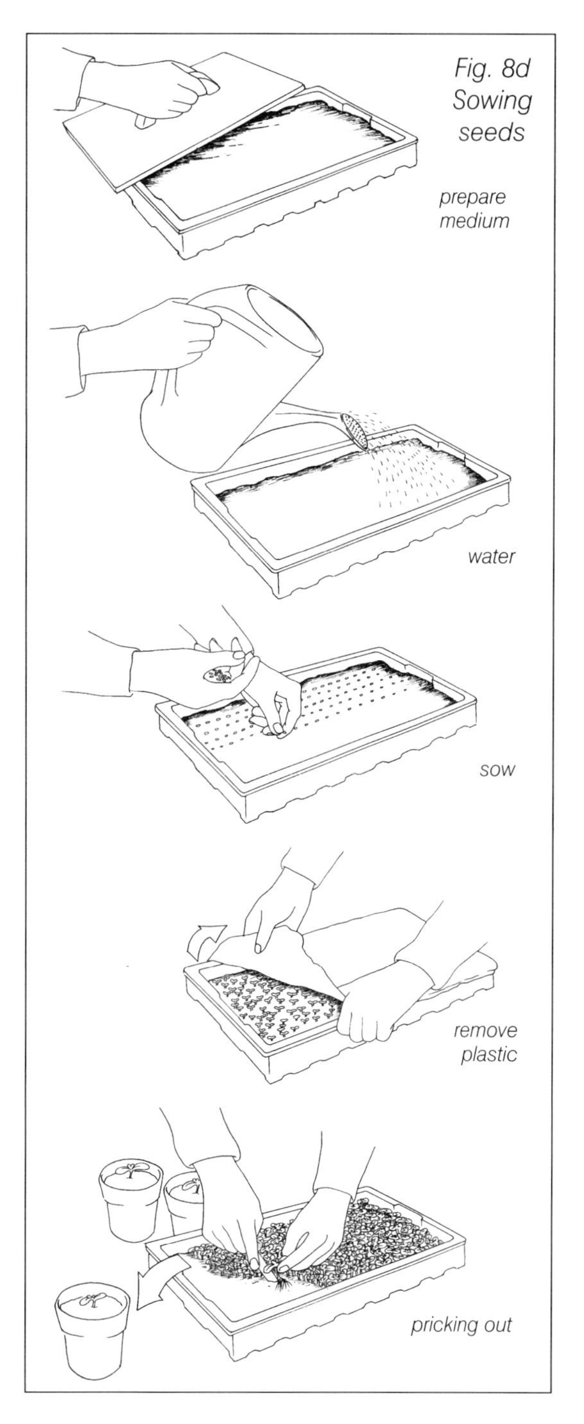

*Fig. 8d Sowing seeds*

## Pricking out, potting on and hardening off

Once the seedlings are large enough to handle easily and have developed a good root system they need to be pricked out.

1. Prepare pots 5-7 cms in diameter or if seedlings are of a small variety prepare further trays. Fill with a soil-based potting compost or weedfree garden soil mixed with compost. Water as above (2).

2. Tease out each seedling gently with a palette knife or lolly stick and transplant each into its own pot.

3. Grow the seedlings on in their pots until the root system is well established. Plant out annuals in early summer and perennials in summer or early autumn when the soil is still warm. Keep well watered and weeded.

4. If the seedlings have been grown in an unheated greenhouse or cold frame they must be gradually hardened off to prevent them from suffering shock from a sudden temperature change. Gradually increase the ventilation so the temperature drops, or leave them in the open for increasing lengths of the day until they are acclimatised.

# CHAPTER 9

# Supplementary Feeding

## Birds

In winter, when the natural food supply for birds becomes scarce and fresh water is hard to obtain, it is important that you supplement their food supply. However, once you start feeding birds it is essential that you provide food and water on a regular basis as they will come to rely on you. If not, the birds will have to compete for an inadequate natural food supply (no matter how many berrying and seeding plants you grow). Birds lose a lot of weight overnight, particularly in cold weather, and lack of food can cause death even to a healthy bird in only a few hours.

Scattering a few scraps of white bread on the lawn will not help the birds much — and will make them susceptible to the threat of prowling cats. So a bird table becomes a basic requirement. The most common visitors are blue tit, chaffinch, blackbird, greenfinch, great tit, dunnock, robin, collared dove, house sparrow, starling and coal tit, but you may also have wren, goldfinch, mistle and song thrush, nuthatch and even the great spotted woodpecker. Over 100 species of bird have been recorded visiting bird tables and feeders. Winter visitors to your garden may include redwing, fieldfare, blackcap and siskin, among others.

### Constructing a bird table

Some birds such as blackbirds, dunnocks and wrens like to forage on the ground for their food, but most birds prefer to feed a few feet off the ground in greater safety. Bird feeding tables can easily be constructed from pieces of wood and should be erected on a stout wooden post or hung in a tree — the latter method is best if you have cat problems — they are less likely to pounce on a swinging table. However, you can take measures to prevent cats climbing the post such as an inverted plastic cone placed halfway up.

*Points to note:*

(a) A roof is not essential. Birds don't object to rain but roofing will keep the food from becoming soggy or covered with snow.

(b) Drainage gaps allow stale food to be scraped away and the table to drain.

(c) The illustration below shows a basic bird table. If squirrels or cats are a problem, you may need to invest in free-standing supports for hanging peanut and seed feeders.

### Siting the table

From your own point of view it is best to site the bird table where you have a good view from your kitchen or living room window. The birds will soon get used to feeding near the house and you will be able to enjoy their antics. It will need to be at least five feet above ground level and near, but not too close, to shrubs and trees so that birds can take cover quickly.

Put food out twice daily — early morning and mid-afternoon and, in very severe weather, even more frequently.

Re-locate the bird table at least once during the winter to reduce the risk of disease and infection. Clear away unwanted or stale food regularly. The table and surrounding ground should be washed regularly.

*Winter bird table*

## Which food for which bird

Seeds for finches, sparrows and tits.

Fruit for thrushes, fieldfares, blackbirds, redwings. Put on the ground.

Nuts for siskins, tits, finches, sparrows.

Meat scraps for starlings.

Fat for tits, woodpeckers, nuthatches.

In severe weather birds will eat almost any food to survive.

## Food to put out

Bones and cooked, but not raw, meat.

Lumps of suet or a fat ball hung up.

Mealworms (from pet shops — keep a supply going in a jar of dry bread flour and bran!).

Smear soft fat or cheese over rough bark on trees or put in holes in logs to attract woodpeckers, tits and nuthatches.

Uncooked pastry and stale cake.

Bread — preferably wholemeal and moistened if old or dry.

Cooked potato, oatmeal, dry porridge oats, fresh coconut, cheese.

Fruit — over-ripe fruit from your fruit bowl.

Raisins, currants, sultanas.

Lodge nuts in crevices in bark or in angular branches — hazel nuts, peanuts (not salted), acorns and beech mast (but not in the breeding season).

Sunflower, niger and other seeds. Many seed mixes are now available but beware nutritionally poor ones containing high proportions of wheat, barley and oats. Ordering from specialist wild bird food suppliers guarantees quality.

Berries collected in summer — rowan, elder, haws, cherries, frozen or stored.

Apples — stored for winter use.

## Devices you can hang from trees, bird tables or free standing feeding stations

Fresh coconut — hung up by string in a tree or from the bird table.

Peanuts and other nuts in a bird feeder, net bag, or purpose made metal grill box. Whole peanuts must not be available during the breeding season.

Scraps of food in a similar basket or bag as above.

Suet log — bore holes in a short length of wooden log and stuff holes with suet (liked by woodpeckers).

Bird pudding stuffed into a yoghurt pot or empty half coconut shell suspended upside down.

## Recipe for bird pudding

Mix together dry cake, cheese (grated), unsalted peanuts, seeds, oatmeal, cold potato or any other scraps in a bowl and pour over melted fat (not oils which don't set at room temperature), and leave to set or stuff while warm and soft into a container to be suspended from string. Proportions roughly 2: 1 scraps: fat.

You can also buy proprietary bird foods — a bit like muesli, but these can be expensive. It is better to buy the individual ingredients and mix with scraps to make your own.

When the ground is really hard and frosty you can help by digging over a small area to turn up all sorts of mini beasts for the birds to feed on.

Space the food types out in your garden. Erect more than one bird table as this allows timid species to feed without victimisation from the aggressive birds who will probably take everything if the food is all in one place!

*A few rules to bird feeding:* Birds can be fed throughout the year. Seedeaters are often very short of food in spring and early summer. Peanuts must be marked as safe, ie free of aflatoxins. Cheap peanuts bought at petshops may well be contaminated and should therefore be avoided. Don't feed salty foods, mouldy foods, desiccated coconut or dried food, which will swell up inside the bird.

Remember that regular, year-round feeding is best.

## Water

It is vital not only to feed birds but to provide a supply of fresh water all year round for them to bathe in and drink. If you have a pond with shallow edges this will be an ideal source of water; if not you can easily make a small bird bath.

Bathing is an important function for birds to help them keep their feathers or plumage in good shape. The feathers insulate the body from the cold and regulate body temperature. Bathing birds have to wet their feathers without soaking them. They then shake themselves and start preening, rubbing oil into their feathers from a special preen gland. This makes them shower proof and by fluffing them up air is trapped to form a good layer of heat insulation.

*Improvised bird bath — hardly elegant but very functional*

You can buy ornamental bird baths. Some of these are not very effective, being made of plastic and hence being too slippery for birds to cope with. Adding rocks or logs will help. If you search hard and are prepared to spend some money you can also obtain beautiful old stone bird baths which sometimes have sculptural qualities. But with a bit of ingenuity you can make your own bird bath which will cost you nothing.

It is essential that you thaw out or break any ice that forms on the bird bath each day. You could go to the expense of installing an aquarium immersion heater and thermostat but make sure it is connected to the mains with suitable outdoor leads or you could electrocute your wildlife (or yourself). Do not add any antifreeze or salt to the water to prevent it freezing!

You could also provide a dust bath, for birds such as sparrows and wrens seem to need to dust bathe and sun bathe to help their feather condition. Mix together fine sand, sifted soil and even sifted ash, in a hollow or even upturned dustbin lid — with drainage holes, and be entertained by the comic antics of dust bathing birds!

## Mammals

Scraps of food that fall from your bird table and hanging feeders will be welcomed by wood mice and voles. You can encourage these nocturnal feeders by putting out food at night, preferably in a cat-proof cage.

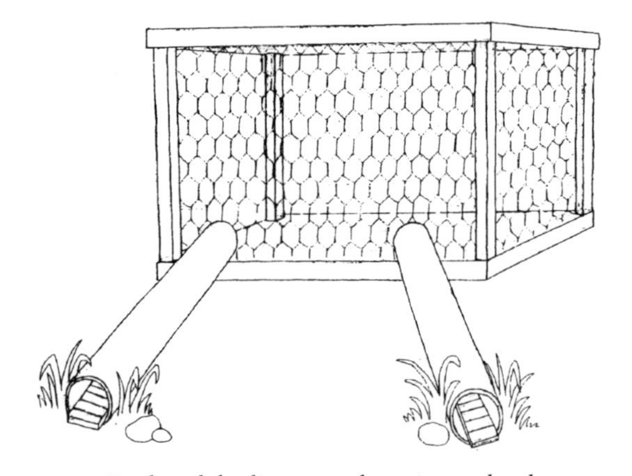

*Enclosed feeding cage for mice and voles*

You may even be lucky enough to attract foxes and even badgers if you live in the right location. That endearing and useful garden friend, the hedgehog, can be attracted by putting out tinned pet food (non-fishy) or scrambled egg. In return your hedgehog will eat garden pests such as slugs.

*Hedgehog*

# CHAPTER 10

# Twelve Things for Wildlife Gardeners to remember!

**1.** Adopt organic gardening methods: (a) Use compost, well rotted down manure, etc., instead of chemical fertilisers. Make your own compost heap. (b) Avoid using pesticides, herbicides, fungicides, algicides. Try companion planting to avoid pest problems in your kitchen garden. (c) Hand weed, where possible, your paths and paved areas and, better still, encourage desirable wildflowers to become established. Remember micro-organisms and invertebrates are needed to maintain a healthy soil structure and chemical treatment can effectively sterilize the soil. (d) Weed selectively — pulling or digging out rampant wildflowers. (e) Never use slug pellets as they may poison birds and hedgehogs.

**2.** Don't be too tidy minded in the garden. Leave areas of long grass and piles of leaves for amphibians, insects, spiders and small mammals to shelter under. Sweep leaves into the hedge bottom or under shrubs if you cannot bear them on your lawn. Leave windfall fruit on the ground to provide a valuable autumn food supply.

**3.** Allow thickets of climbing and rambling shrubs to get established — create a wild corner in your garden with a patch of nettles, brambles and a pile of logs left to rot down.

Nettles are marvellous for the adult red admiral, small tortoiseshell, peacock and comma butterflies to lay their eggs on — the hatching larvae feed on the leaves.

Brambles or blackberry bushes support many insects, the blossom is a good source of pollen for bees and the nectar attracts butterflies such as comma, small tortoiseshell, gatekeeper and peacock. The berries are a useful food for small mammals and birds.

Dead vegetation is a vital ingredient in the wildlife garden. If you leave a pile of logs to rot down gradually you will attract many invertebrates such as spiders, woodwasps and beetles. Fascinating varieties of fungi will soon start the rotting process. These in turn will attract other invertebrates. Even toads, newts and frogs may find shelter in the shade of your wild area. Wild flowers and mosses, ivy and ferns will soon establish themselves to create a visually interesting corner. If it is adjacent to a managed area

*Pile of logs with fungi, hedgehog and thrush with anvil*

of your garden then it will look deliberate, even artistic and not just unkempt!

**4**. Try to plant native trees, shrubs and wildflowers wherever possible. Select ornamental varieties only if they will benefit wildlife in some way. Don't select plants merely for their food-providing qualities — choose those which will encourage animals to breed and become resident in your garden.

**5**. Never dig up any plant from the wild to transplant it into your garden or collect seed from rare or isolated plants. It is in fact illegal to uproot any plant without the permission of the landowner. The aim of wildlife gardening is to create additional habitats and augment the wildflower and native tree and shrub population — not deplete it.

**6**. Never scatter wildflower or garden plant seeds in the countryside. If they do germinate and establish themselves they could lead to crossing of strains, or they could dominate and suppress the indigenous wildflower population which could eventually result in the loss of our native species.

**7**. Don't use peat because peat bogs are being so rapidly destroyed by its wholesale extraction. Alternatives such as coir (coconut waste), garden compost, rockwool (for glasshouses), woodchip for some containerised plants, composted domestic refuse and rotted straw/animal wastes are all increasingly available.

**8**. Buy your seed and wildflower plants from a recognised seed merchant or nursery, certified as using native stock (see list on page 68-70). Introducing similar, but foreign strains could have the same effects as (6).

**9**. Don't disturb nesting mammals or birds by peeping — you may inadvertently trample vegetation near the nest destroying the very cover the bird has chosen. It may make the nest conspicuous to predators such as crows, weasels, rats, magpies, or even other humans. It is also illegal to collect birds' eggs.

**10**. Provide food and water all year round, avoiding whole peanuts when young birds are being fed.

**11**. Keep a seasonal record of what you see and hear in your garden. Send interesting records to your local wildlife trust or biological records centre.

**12**. Finally, find time to relax in your garden and enjoy it!

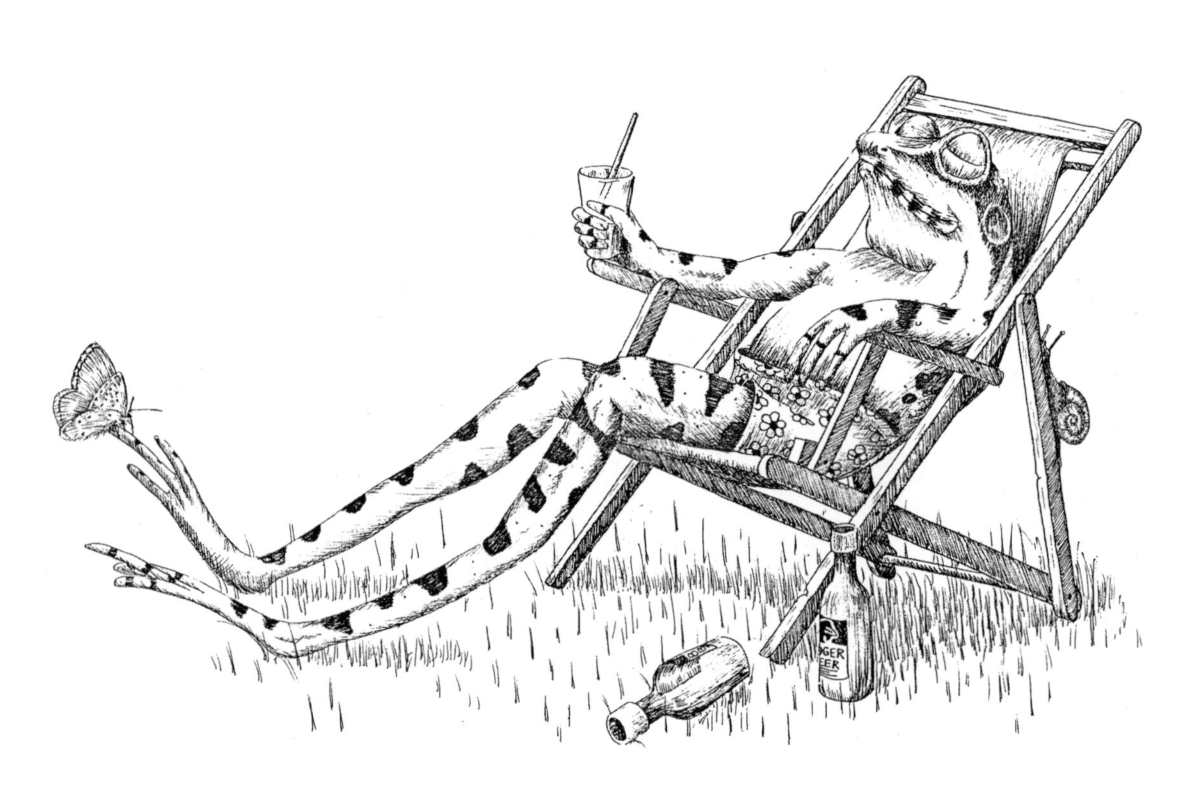

# Useful contacts, references and suppliers

## USEFUL ADDRESSES

**The Wildlife Trusts' national office**
The Wildlife Trusts, The Kiln, Waterside
Newark NG24 1WT
tel. 01636 677711
e-mail: info@wildlife-trusts.cix.co.uk
webpage: www.rsnc.org/main.htm

Addresses for the 46 local wildlife trusts are on the website above or try your telephone directory

**Royal Society for the Protection of Birds**
The Lodge, Sandy SG19 2DL
tel. (01767) 680551
www.rspb.org.uk

**British Trust for Ornithology**
The Nunnery, Thetford IP24 2PU
tel. (01842) 750050
www.bto.org

**Centre for Alternative Technology**
Machynlleth, Powys SY20 9AZ
tel. (0654) 702400
www.cat.org.uk

**Froglife**
Mansion House, 27-28 Market Place, Halesworth
Suffolk IP19 8AY
tel. (01986) 874744 email:
enquiries@tritonhouse.demon.co.uk

**Butterfly Conservation**
Manor Yard, East Lulworth, Wareham, Dorset
BH20 5QP
tel. (01929) 400209
e-mail: butterfly@cix.compulink.co.uk
website: www.butterfly-conservation.org

**Flora Locale**
*(Publishes a list of native provenance wild seed and plant suppliers)*
36 Kingfisher Court, Hambridge Road
Newbury RG14 5SJ
tel. 01635 550380
e-mail: floralocale@naturebureau.co.uk
website: www.floralocale.org

**Plantlife**
21 Elizabeth Street, London SW1W 9RP
tel. (020) 78080100
e-mail: enquiries@plantlife.org.uk
website: www.plantlife.org

**HDRA Henry Doubleday Research Association**
Ryton Organic Gardens, Ryton on Dunsmore,
Coventry CV8 3LG
tel. 024 7630 3517
e-mail enquiry@hdra.org.uk
website: www.hdra.org.uk

**Landlife**
National Wildflower Centre, Court Hey Park,
Liverpool L16 3NA
tel. (0151) 737 1819
email: info@landlife.org.uk
website: www.landlife.org.uk

**The Bat Conservation Trust**
15 Cloisters House, 8 Battersea Park
London SW8 4BG
tel. (020) 76272629
website: www.bats.org.uk

## RECOMMENDED BOOKS

### GENERAL


Chris Baines (2000)
*How to make a wildlife garden* 2nd edition
Frances Lincoln (ISBN 0-7112-1711-4)

Jackie Bennett (1993)
*The wildlife garden month by month*
David & Charles (ISBN 0-7153-0573-5)

Bob and Liz Gibbons (1988)
*Creating a wildlife garden*
Hamlyn/Chancellor Press reprint
(ISBN 1-85152-935-7)


### WILDFLOWERS


Landlife (2000)
*How to make wildflower habitat gardens*
Landlife (ISBN 0-9523472-29)

Landlife (1994)
*Wildflower compendium: A horticultural guide for the wildlife gardener*
Landlife (ISBN 1-899001-05-0)

A. Starling and P. Loosely (1991)
*Wildflowers in the garden*
School Garden Co., Spalding (ISBN 1-85116-806-0)

J. Stevens (1987)
*The National Trust Book of Wildflower Gardening*
Dorling Kindersley, London (ISBN 0-86318-219-4)


### ORGANIC


Geoff Hamilton (1987)
*Successful organic gardening*
Dorling Kindersley, London (ISBN 0-7513-0500-6)

Pauline Pears & Sue Stickland (1999)
*Organic gardening* 2nd edition
Royal Horticultural Society/Mitchell Beazley
(ISBN 1-84000-158-5)


### GARDEN WILDLIFE


Michael Chinery (1986)
*Garden creepy crawlies*
Whittet Books, London (ISBN 1-873580-41-X)

Tom Langton (1997)
*Pond heaven: how to create your own wildlife pond*
BBC Wildlife/Froglife (available from Froglife)

Trevor Beebee (1992)
*Pond Life*
Whittet Books, London (ISBN 0-905483-99-5)

Margaret Vickery (1998)
*Gardening for Butterflies* 2nd edition
Butterfly Conservation, Colchester
(ISBN 0-9522602-6-3)

John Killingbeck (1985)
***Creating and maintaining a garden to attract butterflies***
National Association for Environmental Education
(ISBN 0-907808-12-3)

J. A. Bullock (1992)
***Host plants of British beetles: a list of recorded associations***
Amateur Entomologists' Society
(ISBN 0-900054-56-5)

M. F. Mountain *et al.* (1981)
***Garden plants valuable to bees***
International Bee Research Association
(ISBN 0-8609-8104-5)

Andrew Cannon (1998)
***Garden BirdWatch Handbook***
British Trust for Ornithology, Thetford
(ISBN 0-90379398)

Chris de Feu (1993)
***Nestboxes*** 2nd edition
British Trust for Ornithology, Thetford
(ISBN 0-903793-29-6)

Nigel Matthews (1992)
***Garden for birds***
School Garden Co., Spalding (ISBN 1-85116-805-2)

S. Thompson (1989)
***Bats in the garden***
School Garden Co., Spalding
(ISBN 1-85116-803-6)

R. E. Stebbings and S. T. Walsh (1991)
***Bat Boxes: A guide to the History, Function, Construction and Use in the Conservation of Bats***
3rd edition
Bat Conservation Trust (ISBN 1-872745-02-4)

## WEBPAGES

***Natural gardens;*** *wildlife gardening information and services*
**www.users.zetnet.co.uk/natural**

***Jenny Steel's wildlife garden;*** *on-line garden with information and course details*
**www.wildlife-gardening.co.uk**

***Graham's paradise garden***; *on-line garden with wildlife gardening information*
**www.maigold.co.uk**

***Flora for Fauna*** *list of native plants according to postcode and list of suppliers of native provenance seeds and plants*
**www.nhm.ac.uk/fff**

***'Gardenlink'*** *to other gardening and wildlife websites:*
**www.gardenlinks.ndo.co.uk/wildlife.htm**

***Anglia Multimedia;*** *study ideas based around wildlife in school wildlife garden*
**www.anglia.co.uk/angmulti/garden/**

***BBC gardening pages;*** *queries, suppliers and 'garden finder':*
**www.bbc.co.uk/gardening**
**www.gardenersworld.com**

***Irish peatland campaign*** *with information on peat alternatives, composting and various gardening topics*
**www.ipcc.ie/wildlifegardening.html**

***Soil Association***
**www.soilassociation.org**

***Royal Horticultural Society***
**www.rhs.org.uk**

## SUPPLIERS OF PLANTS, SEEDS AND WATER PLANTS

### LISTS OF NATIVE PROVENANCE SUPPLIERS

**The Good Bulb Guide** is a list of reputable bulb suppliers published by:
Flora & Fauna International, Great Eastern House, Tenison Rd, Cambridge CBI 2TT
tel. (01223) 571000
e-mail: info@fauna-flora.org

**Flora for Fauna** (list of native provenance seed and plant suppliers)
website: www.nhm.ac.uk/fff

**Flora Locale** (list of native provenance seed and plant suppliers)
36 Kingfisher Court, Hambridge Road
Newbury RG14 5SJ
tel. 01635 550380
e-mail: floralocale@naturebureau.co.uk
website: www.floralocale.org

### NATIVE WILDFLOWER, SEED AND TREE SUPPLIERS

**Ashton Wold Wildflowers**
Ashton Wold, Peterborough, Cambs PE8 5LZ
tel. (01832) 273575

**The British Native Species Centre**
Grange Farm, Grange Road, Widmer End
High Wycombe, Buckinghamshire HPI5 6AE
tel. (01494) 718203

**British Seed Houses Ltd**
Bewsey Industrial Estate, Pitt Street, Warrington, Cheshire WA5 5LE
tel. (01925) 654411
e-mail: seeds@bshwarr.co.uk
*seeds only*

**British Trees and Shrubs**
125 Hansford Square, Combe Down, Bath
Avon BA2 5LL
tel. (01225) 840080
e-mail: plants@britishtrees.co.uk

**British Wild Flower Plants**
31 Main Road, North Burlingham
Norwich NR13 4TA
tel. (01603) 716615
e-mail: linda@wildflowers.co.uk
www.wildflowers.co.uk

**BTCV Enterprises Conservation Centre**
Balby Road, Doncaster, South Yorkshire
DN4 0RH
tel. (01302) 859522

**Chiltern Seeds**
Bortree Stile, Ulverston, Cumbria LA12 7PB
tel. (0129) 581173

**Christie-Elite Nurseries**
Forres, Moray IV36 0TW
tel. (01309) 672633
e-mail: celite@globalnet.co.uk

**Country Flowers Wild Flower Nursery**
62 Lower Sands, Dymchurch, Romney Marsh
Kent TN29 0NF
tel. (01303) 873052

**Eco-seeds**
1 Bar View Cottages, Shore Road, Strangford
County Down BT30 7NN
tel. (02844) 881227
e-mail: eco-seeds@strangford.fsnet.co.uk

**Emorsgate Seeds**
Terrington St. Clement, Kings Lynn
Norfolk PE34 4NY
tel. (01553) 829028

**Heritage Seeds**
Osmington, Weymouth, Dorset DT3 6EX
tel. (01305) 834504

**W. W. Johnson & Sons Ltd**
London Road, Boston, Lincolnshire PE21 9AD
tel. (01205) 365051

**John Chambers Wildflower Seeds**
15 Westleigh Road, Barton Seagrave, Kettering
Northamptonshire NN15 5AJ
tel. (01933) 652562

**John Shipston Bulbs**
Y Felin, Hellan Armgoed, Whitland
Camarthanshire SA34 0SL
tel. (01994) 240125
e-mail: bluebell@200.co.uk
*specialist wildflower plugs and bulbs*

**Mike Handyside Wild Flowers**
15 The Old Paddock, Main Road, Goostrey
Crewe, Cheshire CW4 8QZ
tel. (01477) 549336
*specialist for wildflower plugs and bulbs*

**Landlife**
National Wildflower Centre, Court Hey Park
Liverpool L16 3NA
tel. (0151) 737 1819
email: info@landlife.org.uk
www.landlife.org.uk

**London Wildlife Garden Centre**
(London Wildlife Trust), 28 Marsden Road
London SE15
tel. (020) 7252 9186

**Meadowlands**
The Park Lodge, Park Avenue, Wortley
South Yorkshire S30 7DR
tel. (0114) 2830322
e-mail: meadowlands@dial.pipex.com

**Mires Beck Nursery**
Low Mill Lane, North Cave, Brough
East Yorkshire HU15 2NR
tel. (01430) 421543

**Mike Thorne**
Wild Seeds, Branas, Llandefel, Gwynedd LL23 7RF
tel. (01678) 530427
*seeds only*

**Naturescape**
Langar, Nottinghamshire NG13 9EP
tel. (01949) 860592
e-mail: sales@naturescape.co.uk

**Organic Trees**
Doire-na-Mairst, Morvern, By Oban
Argyll PA34 5XE
tel. (01967) 421203

**Poyntzfield Herb Nursery**
Black Isle, By Dingwall, Ross & Cromarty
IV7 8LX
tel. (01381) 610352

**Really Wild Flowers**
Spring Mead, Bedchester, Shaftesbury
Dorset SP7 0JU
tel. (01747) 811778
email: rwflowers@aol.com

**Suffolk Herbs**
Monks Farm, Coggleshall Road, Kelvedon
Essex C05 9PG
tel. (01376) 572456

**Touchwood Tree Nursery**
Shay Lodge Farm, Burbage, Buxton
Derbyshire SK17 6TS
tel. (01298) 70441

**Ulster Native Trees/Wildwood Trees**
67 Temple Rise, Templepatrick, Ballyclare
Co. Antrim BT39 0AG
tel. (028) 9443 3068

**The Wildflower Centre**
Church Farm, Sisland, Norwich
Norfolk NR14 6EF
tel. (01508) 520235

**YSJ Seeds**
Kingfield Conservation Nursery, Springbank
Broadenham Lane, Winsham, Chard
Somerset TA20 4JF
tel. (01460) 30070
e-mail: ysjseeds@aol.com

SPECIALIST BUTTERFLY PLANTS SUPPLIERS:

**Paul Batty**
4 Byron Rd, Dinnington, Sheffield S25 2LP
tel. (01909) 550272

**Mike Mullis**
27 Stream Farm Cottages, Netherfield Road, Battle
East Sussex TN33 0HH
tel. (01424) 773092

SPECIALIST POND PLANT SUPPLIERS:

**Merton Hall Pond Ltd**
Merton, Thetford, Norfolk IP25 6QH
tel. (01953) 881763
e-mail: triton@globalnet.co.uk
website: www.mhp-ltd.co.uk

**Stapeley Water Gardens Ltd**
Stapeley, Nantwich, Cheshire CW5 7LH
tel. (01270) 623868
e-mail: stapeleywg@btinternet.com

**Water Garden Nursery**
High Croft, Morrend, Wembworthy, Chumleigh
Devon EX 18 7SG
tel. (01837) 83566

**Wildwoods Water Gardens Ltd**
Theobolds Road, Crews Hill, Enfield,
Middlesex EN2 9BP
tel. (020) 83660243
e-mail: info@wildwoods.co.uk

## SUPPLIERS and MANUFACTURERS
of equipment for wildlife gardens and ponds

Sourcebook listing suppliers, books and manufacturers of wildlife gardening products:
Ron Wilson (1998)
*Gardening for wildlife enjoyment*
Wild Boar Books (ISBN 1-899898-08-5)

BIRD FOOD, VARIOUS BOXES, FEEDERS AND SCHWEGLER WOODCRETE NESTBOXES

**CJ WildBird Foods**
The Rea, Upton Magna, Shrewsbury SY4 4UB
tel. (0800) 7312820 fax 01743 709504
e-mail: sales@birdfoodco.uk
website: www.birdfood.co.uk

**Bamfords Ltd**
Globe Mill, Midge Hall Lane, Midge Hall
Leyland PR5 3TN
tel. (01772) 456300
e-mail: sales@bamfords.co.uk

**Jacobi Jayne & Co**
Hawthorn Cottage, Maypole, Hoath, Canterbury
Kent CT3 4LW
tel. 01227 860388

**Ernest Charles & Co Ltd**
Copplestone Mills, Copplestone, Crediton
Devon EX17 5NF
tel. (01363) 94942 fax (01363) 84147

*feeders and boxes for butterflies, lacewings, ladybirds:*

**Biotal Industrial Products Ltd**
5 Chiltern Close, Cardiff CF4 5DL
tel. 029 2074 7414 fax 029 2074 7140
e-mail: bip@biotal.co.uk

POND LINERS

**Bradshaws**
Clifton Industrial Estate, York Y03 8XX
tel. 01904 691169

**Butyl Products**
11 Radford Crescent, Billericay, Essex CM12 0DW
tel. (01277) 653281

**CPS Aquatic**
28 Riverside Gardens, Langford, Biggleswade
Beds SG18 9RZ
tel. (01462) 700507

**Fawcetts Tarpaulins**
Liner Dept, Freepost, Back Lane, Longton PR4 5JA
tel. 01772 612125

**Midland Butyl Ltd**
Windmill Hill, Biggin Lane, Nr Hulland Ward
Ashbourne, Derbys DE5 3FN
tel. (01335) 372133

**Monarflex**
Lyon Way, Hatfield Road, St Albans,
Hertfordshire AL4 0LB
tel. (01727) 830116

**Sussex Aquatic Services**
Sussex Country Gardens, Newhaven Road
Kingston, Lewes, East Sussex BN7 3NE
tel. (01273) 477620

*Bentonite clay liners:*

**Rawell Water Control Systems Ltd**
Carr Lane, Hoylake, Merseyside CH47 4FE
tel. (0151) 6325771

COMPOSTING

*Where to buy peat-free products* leaflet available from The Wildlife Trusts National Office (page 67) or ask your local Trust for details.

**Original Organics**
Unit 9, Langlands Business Centre, Uffculme
Devon EX15 3DA
tel. (01884) 841515

*wormery*

**Wiggly Wrigglers**
Lower Blakemore Farm, Blakemere, Herefordshire
HR2 9PX
tel. freephone 0800 216990
e-mail: orders@wigglywrigglers.co.uk
website: www.wigglywrigglers.co.uk

ORGANIC, SUSTAINABLE AND LOW IMPACT GARDENING PRODUCTS

**Organic Gardening Catalogue**
Riverdene Business Park, Molesey Road, Hersham
Surrey KT12 4RG
free tel. 01932 253666
e-mail: chaseorg@aol.com